This volume is the sixth of a number in which are being published the results of research carried on by the faculty and research scholars working at Yale University in the field of Foreign Area Studies. In 1953 there was published *The Multi-State System of Ancient China* by Richard L. Walker and in 1954 there were published *The Russian Hexameter* by Richard T. Burgi and *China's March Toward the Tropics* by Herold J. Wiens, followed in 1960 by the *Index to Ch'ing Tai Ch'ou Pan I Wu Shih Mo*, edited by David Nelson Rowe, and in 1961 by *Britain's Imperial Role in the Red Sea Area 1800-1878* by Thomas E. Marston. Subsequent volumes will include studies in the various disciplines, both Humanities and Social Sciences, in respect to East Asia, Southeast Asia and the Soviet Union. The undersigned are acting as general editors for the purpose of securing and approving the best possible results of research in these fields at Yale. In the various disciplines or areas to which the special skills of this committee do not directly apply, it is planned to secure supplementary advice from both inside and outside the University.

DAVID NELSON ROWE
Chairman, Editorial Committee
Professor of Political Science

WILLIAM S. CORNYN
Professor of Slavic and
Burmese Languages

KARL J. PELZER
Professor of Geography

VLADIMIR PETROV

WHAT
CHINA
POLICY
?

SHOE STRING PRESS

HAMDEN, CONN.

Library of Congress Catalog Card No. 61-17805

Printed in the United States of America

"While I do not believe that the United States should recognize Communist China at the present time in view of their continued belligerence and offensive manners, I do not believe it is wise to continue to ignore 600,000,000 people on the China mainland in the naive belief that they will somehow go away."

SENATOR J. W. FULBRIGHT, *Chairman*,
Senate Foreign Relations Committee.
Reported in the *New York Times* on
November 1, 1959.

TABLE OF CONTENTS

FOREWORD   ix

PART ONE

The United States Policy of Nonrecognition of
    Communist China   3
International Law and International Morality   8
Consequences of Recognition   18
Recognition and Disarmament   33
Who Should Represent China in the United Nations   38
The Price of Recognition   40
Sino-Soviet Rift   50
Prospects   60

PART TWO

Chinese Representation in the United Nations   75
The History   78
Criteria for Representation   84
Representation *vs.* Recognition   89
Credentials   91
New Trends in the United Nations   95
Realities of the United Nations   103
Alternatives   110
New Trends in the United States   116

CONCLUSIONS   129

NOTES

Part One   133
Part Two   139

FOREWORD

Among the issues which plague our world, the world torn apart by the conflict between the communist East and democratic West, there are several which have become chronic. Unsolved, and often unsoluble, they stay dormant for months and years then suddenly erupt, splashing over the front pages of newspapers and making good people everywhere worry lest the fight over these issues would end up in a nuclear holocaust. One such issue is that of Communist China, its "legitimate interests" in Asia, and its "rightful place" among the world powers. Unlike its senior partner, the Soviet Union, which successfully entered the international arena as a major power during the last war, Communist China remains in a political quarantine, "ignored" by the majority of nations. After twelve years of effective control over the mainland of China, the Peking government is still denied admission to that international club, the United Nations, to which even the smallest and the newest nations can belong.

This isolation — "containment" would be another word for it — has been possible due largely to the efforts of the United States and its allies who, for a wide variety of reasons, withhold recognition from the militantly revolutionary regime of China. The stakes involved here have come to transgress regional, economic, political and even ideological considerations. The problem of international recognition of Communist China has acquired a symbolic significance in the gigantic struggle between the visibly irreconcilable, implacably hostile camps, a significance appreciated even by those who stay out — or think that they stay out — of that struggle. The "Chinese issue" has acquired its chronic character through sheer intensity of feelings on both sides and, in the process, turned into one of the sorest spots in relations among nations. Yet, the resistance to any change in *status quo* appears formidable, for such a change would be immediately hailed as a great victory by the one side and would have to be accepted as a humiliating defeat by the other.

Few people would question that international acceptance of the Peking regime is in the interests of the communist bloc which — without a single dissenting voice — has for years been clamoring for such an acceptance. However, there has been no similar unity of opinion on this subject in the non-communist world, where the policy of "containment" of Communist China has often been criticized on different grounds by many individuals, political parties and governments. Such criticism has been harsher whenever the Chinese problem has been viewed in isolation, apart from the global context of the Cold War. At times, attacks on Western — primarily American — intransigence in its China policy have been made from irresponsible or ill-informed sources. On other occasions they have been launched from perfectly respectable and highly qualified quarters. It is a purpose of this study to systematize the arguments, as they have been formulated by the most authoritative sources *for* and *against* recognition of Communist China. Another task is to present the issue of Chinese representation in the United Nations. Here, in a separate chapter, the reader will find different and opposing views on this extremely intricate problem.

An honest effort has been made by the author to give each side an opportunity to airs its arguments — which are given in their original form. Out of many books, statements and articles the author has selected what he believes to be the clearest and most convincing passages containing the essence of the arguments.

The Chinese issue has clearly become a partisan one, and not only in the United States. It was impossible for the author to abstain entirely from expressing his opinions or passing his judgment on the validity of some statements. The almost thirty years that he had lived in the Soviet Union prior to his arrival in the United States led him to feel that there cannot be any impartiality in discussion of a problem of vital importance to the fortunes of one's nation. Partiality, however, need not be confused with a lack of objectivity. If this work would help to clear up some misconceptions surrounding the problem and enable the reader to form an informed opinion on it, its purpose would be well achieved.

VLADIMIR PETROV

July 1961
Yale University

WHAT CHINA POLICY?

Part One

THE UNITED STATES POLICY OF NONRECOGNITION OF COMMUNIST CHINA

The controversy over the refusal by the United States to recognize the communist government of China is as old as that government itself. It may be, as some feel, that "the importance of the recognition has been grossly exaggerated by many Americans" and that "extreme views overstate the importance of recognition policy and tend to obscure the long-term problem of dealing with Communist China."[1] Still, despite the multitude of arguments advanced by proponents of recognition, the chances for it at the moment appear hardly greater than they were at the time of the Round Table Conference on American Policy Toward China held by the Department of State in October 1949.

The public at large had taken the defeat of the Nationalist forces in China as a major defeat of American Far Eastern policy. The efforts of the administration and of a considerable section of the press, who had for several years tried to prepare the public for the inevitability of the collapse of the Chiang Kai-shek regime, proved to be in vain. In retrospect, it seems that the Department of State had grossly underestimated the public anti-communist sentiment and overestimated the success of its systematic efforts to put the blame for what happened in China on the Nationalists. The reaction to the White Paper on China published by the Department of State in August 1949, indicting the "reactionary clique of the Kuomintang" and putting Chiang on notice that no further American aid would be forthcoming, was bitter and overwhelming. The government, supported only by scattered liberal voices, tried to scoff at the criticism and to ascribe it to the machinations of what had been loosely described as the "China Lobby." It kept repeating that the "corrupt Kuomintang regime" deserved no sympathy. "What has happened in my judgment," Secretary Acheson was saying early in 1950, "is

3

that the almost inexhaustible patience of the Chinese people in their misery ended. They did not bother to overthrow this government. There was really nothing to overthrow. . . . They completely withdrew their support from this government, and when this support was withdrawn, the whole military establishment disintegrated. . . . The Communists did not create this condition. . . . They did not create a great force which moved out from under Chiang Kai-shek. But they were shrewd and cunning to mount it, to ride this thing into victory and into power."[2]

Such explanations, whatever their merits, had little effect. The criticism remained vociferous. It reflected strong historical and emotional ties between America and China — the traditional China, where due, partly at least, to the past efforts of American diplomacy no single alien power had exercised predominant influence. The reaction in the United States reflected the dangers of what can happen to a government which attempts to separate its foreign policy from domestic considerations in a situation when public indignation is aroused. Theoretically, at least, such a separation can be feasible. As Professor Quincy Wright puts it:

> Foreign policy differs from domestic policy in that its implementation depends on conditions little subject to the control of national law and little understood by the national public. Foreign policy must, therefore, often adapt to conditions which public opinion chooses to ignore or of which it is unaware.[3]

In actual practice, however, a government — especially that of a democratic country — has to be aware of the domestic political risks involved.[4]

For a few critical months the Truman administration persisted in its evaluation of what had happened in China.[6] "There is every evidence," says Quincy Wright, that early in 1950 "the United States was preparing to recognize the Communist Government," and he adds that "in retrospect it seems unfortunate that recognition was not accorded at that time."[6]

Under a closer investigation, the evidence Wright is talking about does not appear conclusive. It is true that in the Department of State there prevailed a strongly anti-Chiang sentiment and that the government was prepared to deal with the new regime: one

4

indication was that it did not close down U.S. missions and consulates in China until their operations were made impossible by constant pressure and abuse on the part of the communists. It also avoided resuming aid to Chiang Kai-shek, apparently considering such aid futile. But while "waiting for the dust to settle," U.S. spokesmen kept blasting away at communism in general, and at "Soviet imperalism" which supposedly dominated the Chinese Communists in particular. It is possible that these speeches were designed for internal consumption only, in order to show that the government was not getting soft on communism. However, there are indications that Truman could not make up his mind as to what to do. For instance, when Secretary-General of the United Nations, Trygve Lie, went to Washington in April 1950 to ask for at least tacit support for unseating the Chiang representatives in that organization, Truman turned him down, declaring that "nobody can trust the communists."[7] On the whole it seems that recognition of the Peking regime at that time was ruled out by domestic political developments. Even as it was, the public was sufficiently aroused to bring about the defeat of the Democratic Party in the congressional elections of 1950 in which the administration's China policy was a major issue. And Joseph G. Whalen of The Library of Congress says:

> Probably no foreign policy in many years has split the nation's body politic so deeply as the "loss" of China. . . . Criticism covered the whole range of the Truman Administration's treatment of Communism, both domestically and internationally, and became the central issue in the Presidential campaign of 1952.[8]

This may support Wright's contention that the most suitable time for recognition of Communist China was early in 1950, when Mao Tse-tung's regime was recognized by a number of countries outside of the communist bloc.[9] What made the problem so formidable thereafter was the communist aggression in Korea in June of the same year, and a strong feeling in the United States that Communist China, along with the Soviet Union, had been behind the North Korean attack. The events confirmed these suspicions[10] and furnished the American public with abundant grounds for detesting Communist China.

It is doubtful whether early American diplomatic recognition, by itself, would have deterred the Chinese Communists from backing the North Korean aggression and from their own subsequent intervention in Korea. In fact, had recognition been granted, the position of the United States in the conflict would have been much more complicated. It would have been more difficult to rally public opinion at home in order to fight communism in Korea after an even further more humiliating defeat of American policy in China. The "disengagement" concept in the Far East, initially advocated by some military leaders in the Pentagon, would have likely become an integral part of United States policy and one may speculate that the Truman "police action" would not have been undertaken at all.[11] In addition, one can safely assume that in the absence of the American objections, a Chinese Communist representative would be sitting, along with a Soviet one, in the Security Council of the United Nations. Under such circumstances, to mobilize that organization against the aggressor in Korea would have been impossible.

The way the Korean war was fought brought heavy casualties to American troops. In the United States it caused wide-spread indignation, particularly over the "Manchurian privileged sanctuary," and led to the bitter MacArthur controversy. The wild communist charges of bacteriological warfare and the atrocities that the communists inflicted upon American POWs and Korean civilians added fuel to the fire. Nobody in the United States talked about "agrarian reformers" of China any more. In all, the psychological climate in the country became such as to make any discussion about recognizing the Peking regime politically unrealistic, to say the least.

The following years have brought little to alleviate the situation. If anything, the image of Communist China as an aggressive and arrogant power has been strengthened. The invasion of Tibet in 1951, the violations of the Korean and Indochina armistices and of the 1955 agreement on repatriation of American citizens, the crises over the off-shore islands in 1954 and 1958, all had their effect. Taiwan was proclaimed indispensable to the United States defense; aid to Chiang Kai-shek was resumed. Although the Nationalists were "put on a leash," the island itself was put under the protection of the United States Navy on Truman's orders. The mutual defense treaty with the Republic of China went into effect in 1955 and the situation in the Far East seemed to stabilize itself. This arrangement, although admittedly not an ideal one, seemed to satisfy the American public. The voices demanding the abandonment of Chiang Kai-shek to his fate became silent: from now on the preservation of the Nationalists became good foreign policy — and good politics.

This may explain why United States policy toward China has been attacked by relatively few critics at home. "Opinion in the United States favorable to recognition," said Wright in 1957, "is supported by no propaganda organizations and by no audible voices in the government. It is represented by some writers on international law and relations and by occasional business men and journalists. . . ."[12]

Nevertheless, the "long-term problem of dealing with Communist China" is with us today as it was ten years ago. Its significance is difficult to exaggerate. More than six hundred million Chinese are still controlled by the communist regime, the very existence of which accounts for major outlays in the United States military budget, for extended and burdensome military and economic aid programs, and for disagreements between the United States and many governments of Europe, Asia and Africa as to how to deal with China. Moreover, the direction of American policy toward China seriously affects official thinking in matters reaching far beyond the Far East. It affects the American position in the United Nations, the problems of arms control and disarmament, the attitude toward the Soviet bloc, the system of American defense alliances. Indeed, it would be difficult to find an aspect of United States foreign policy which would not, in one way or another, be affected by considerations related to Communist China. These considerations have been so overwhelming that at times it appeared doubtful whether the United States has remained master of its policies or has reduced its freedom of action to a point when every move is virtually forced upon it by circumstances beyond its control and where there is no more room for maneuver.

With the advent of the new administration in Washington, and because of the admitted inclination on the part of some leading Democrats towards a change in American Far Eastern policy, it might be advisable to review the arguments for and against recognition. These arguments can be divided into three groups: a) Those which deal with formal, legal aspects of the problem and with the traditional American view on recognition of new governments; b) Those which deal with the likely effects of recognition of Communist China on the situation in the Far East and Southeast Asia; and c) Those which deal with the problems transcending possible developments in the Western Pacific. This latter group has to be considered separately because of the highly speculative nature of the arguments involved. The differences of approach in group "b" are essentially those of degree and result from different evaluations of established facts. The arguments which we include in group "c" should more properly be classified as products of imaginative intellectual exercise and the emotional predisposition of the critics. Nonetheless, both attempt to answer the general question: Should the United States recognize Communist China as a matter of sound policy? Somewhat apart, but closely related, is the question whether the United States should accede to the demands of a growing group of nations and allow Communist China to be seated in the General Assembly and the Security Council of the United Nations.

In the final section of this chapter we will review some of the proposals on a new approach to Communist China, including those which emerged after the inauguration of the Kennedy administration. At first glance, these proposals may appear limited in scope. Yet, in evaluating them we shall keep in mind that any significant change in policy toward China would inevitably lead to an over-all revision of the structure of United States foreign policy, especially of that overwhelming part of it which deals with the problems of the Cold War.

INTERNATIONAL LAW AND INTERNATIONAL MORALITY

The legal argument that the United States should grant recognition to the Communist Government of China simply on the ground that the latter had established effective control over the mainland of China is probably the oldest. It is also one of the least conclusive because for every authority on international law favoring automatic recognition of a *de facto* government there is at least one insisting that the recognition must be a matter of political judgment. Quincy Wright, one of the foremost proponents of recognition, likes to quote a passage from Judge Hersh Lauterpacht, who said:

> The emphasis — and the emphasis is a constant feature of diplomatic correspondence — on the principle that the existence of a state (or of a government) is a question of fact signifies that, whenever the necessary factual requirements exist, the granting of recognition is a matter of legal duty.[13]

However, Stanley K. Hornbeck, a career diplomat and an international lawyer, pointing out the continued existence of the Nationalist Government of China on Chinese territory, quotes another paragraph from the same work of Lauterpacht which, in his judgment, nullifies the paragraph favored by Wright:

> So long as the lawful government offers resistance which is not ostensibly hopeless or purely nominal, the *de jure* recognition of the revolutionary party as a government constitutes premature recognition which the lawful government is entitled to regard as an act of intervention contrary to international law. . . . Premature recognition is a tortious act against the legal government; it is a breach of international law.[14]

Whether the Nationalists' resistance is "purely nominal" is, of course, a matter of individual judgment. Since some grave doubts have been expressed on that score, the opponents of recognition (and United States government legal experts) are inclined to favor the approach of L. Oppenheim, who states:

> Recognition will, as a rule be given without any conditions, provided the new State is safely and permanently established. Since, however, the granting of recognition is a matter of policy, and not of law, nothing prevents an old State from making the recognition of a new State dependent upon the latter fulfilling certain conditions.[15]

Professor T. C. Chen considers highly deplorable the use of recognition of a new *State* as means of extracting concessions. But he views the situation quite differently when it is a question of recognition of a new government, for, according to T. C. Chen, "recognition of governments must be considered as an entirely different matter from the recognition of States."[16] He proceeds to quote Professor Smith's conclusions regarding British practice:

> It is clear that the question of recognition is fundamentally a question of policy rather than a question of law. This is to say, there is no such thing as a "right" to recognition, and every State is entitled to grant or withhold the recognition. . . of a new Government, upon grounds of policy which must necessarily be determined by itself.[17]

This position has been taken by most American Secretaries of State in modern times whenever recognition of a new government has been in doubt for political or moral reasons. Wright's assertion that recognition of Communist China "would be in accord with [American] traditional policy and the normal expectations of international law" is further disputed by Ambassador Hornbeck:

> The principles and criteria to be applied to the question of according diplomatic recognition are many, and sound policy-making calls for weighing not only physical and political facts but legal *and* moral *and social* considerations together with a careful estimate of probable consequences. . . . While it may or may not imply moral approbation, it does certify to political acceptance by the according state, does give the recipient state or government a legal status.[18]

And Secretary Dulles states flatly:

> There is nothing automatic about recognition.[19]

The legal argument was summed up by Pitman B. Potter, editor of the American Journal of International Law:

> The present writer would fully admit, after a good deal of investigation and reflection, that the older international law concerning recognition was somewhat unsatisfactory on all essential points. . . . It can therefore be said that the states of the world today are completely free to recognize or refuse to recognize Communist China.[20]

* * *

10

More controversal has been a question whether the communist regime is sufficiently stable in exercising its control over the population. Closely tied to this is another question, namely, whether the communist government is truly representative of the Chinese people. Back in 1792, Thomas Jefferson wrote that "it accords with our principles to acknowledge any government to be rightful which is formed by the will of the nation, substantially declared."[21] Is this the case in China today? Is recognition still premature, as so many people felt in 1950, or has the communist regime passed the test of stability? Opinions here differ widely. For example, Professor Richard L. Walker reports that in 1957 there were signs of widespread unrest on the mainland of China.[22] At the same time, Quincy Wright states:

> Information available on the internal situation of China indicates that the Peking Government enjoys greater political stability. . . and popular approval than any government which China has had for centuries in spite of its use of dictatorial and brutal methods applied internally and of aggression, treaty breaches, and violations of international law externally.[23]

On the other hand, some students of China observe considerable instability under the cloak of strength the communists present to the outside world. Professor David Nelson Rowe says:

> Today there seems little reason to doubt that the Chinese Communists are gradually but steadily working themselves into a problem of internal dissidence so massive that the mere slowness of its development may deceive us into unawareness of it. . . . It is the task of a sophisticated economic and political warfare, backed up by constant military readiness, to aid and abet the development of massive dissidence among the suffering Chinese people.[25]

A view that nonrecognition is a legitimate instrument of foreign policy is expressed by Professor K. C. Wheare who states:

> [The President] has the power. . . . to recognize new governments or not to recognize them, and this power he has exercised very many times on his own responsibility. 'At times, indeed,' says Professor Corwin, 'this prerogative has proved a most potent instrument of foreign policy,' a remark which applies as well to its non-use as to its use.

11

President Wilson encompassed the downfall of Huerta's regime in Mexico in 1915 by refusing to recognize it as even a government *de facto,* and the pivotal feature of our relations with both Mexico and Russia for some years was the refusal of successive administrations at Washington to recognize as *de jure* the governments of these countries.[26]

Nonrecognition, of course, could be only one of many factors which can affect the stability of the regime in question. It does not have to be necessarily a decisive factor. But the United States government has held that it can add substantially to the instability of the already unstable regime, as that of Communist China:

> The United States holds the view that Communism's rule in China is not permanent and that it one day will pass. By withholding diplomatic recognition from Peiping it seeks to hasten that passing. . . . The United States is convinced that the Chinese Communist regime does not represent the true will or aspirations of the Chinese people.[27]

The question of whether the communist regime represents the will of the Chinese people has been considered by the United States, at least outwardly, to be of major importance. In 1951 Assistant Secretary of State for Far Eastern Affairs Dean Rusk said:

> The peace and security of China are being sacrificed to the ambitions of the Communist conspiracy. . . . We can tell our friends in China that the United States will not acquiesce in the degradation which is being forced upon them. . . . We do not recognize the authorities in Peking for what they pretend to be. . . . It is not the Government of China. It does not speak for China in the community of nations. We recognize the National Government of the Republic of China, even though the territory under its control is severely restricted. We believe it more authentically represents the views of the great body of the Chinese people.[28]

Six years later, a new Assistant Secretary of State for Far Eastern Affairs, Walter S. Robertson, stated:

> The defiant imposters in Peiping come no closer to representing the true interests, aspirations, and will of the Chinese people than William Z. Foster comes to representing the will and aspirations of the American people. Their

regime was imposed by force. . . . It has been kept in power by bloody purges and the liquidation of some 18 million of mainland Chinese in 7 years. Our government is opposed to any action which would betray the hopes of those having the will to resist it.[29]

This language obviously reflects the bitterness of the struggle the United States has been engaged in and resentment over its inability to be always on the winning side. Back in 1923 when the United States still felt well protected by two oceans and was conscious of its great and growing power, it could take a more detached view attaching little importance to the popularity of governments in other lands:

While this government has laid stress upon the value of expressed popular approval in determining whether a new government should be recognized, it has never insisted that the will of the people of a foreign State may not be manifested by long continued acquiescence in a regime actually functioning as a government. [Such view should not be considered] a derogation of the democratic ideals cherished by our people.[30]

We notice a repeated recurrence of strong moral overtones in many writings on foreign policy. But is there a moral issue involved? If the communist regime in China is immoral, does it mean that we put the stamp of approval on it by extending to it our recognition? How much prestige do we add to this regime by the mere act of recognition? We find here, again, that the views of the proponents and the opponents of the recognition are at extreme opposites. Former chief American negotiator in Panmunjom, Arthur H. Dean, says:

There is no doubt that recognition does enhance the prestige of the government recognized and is of value for this reason. . . . Whether or not it also signifies political and moral approval of the government recognized is an issue which lies at the very heart of the controversy.[31]

Dean himself believes that morality has nothing to do with diplomatic recognition:

Formal recognition of a government is merely recognition of fact of its effective control, of its intention to act as

13

sovereign and of its ability to carry out its mandates. Moral approval is not involved.[32]

Quincy Wright goes considerably further:

> The charge that the Communist Government of China should not be recognized because it is communistic, totalitarian, dictatorial, brutal, and therefore immoral. . . cannot be sustained. The nonrecognition of a government for the purpose of influencing the form of the government, economy, culture, or ideology of another state amounts. . . to intervention in the domestic affairs of that state and violates a basic principle of international morality and international law.[33]

Such a view, however, is a rarity among the experts on international law. Whether withholding recognition necessarily hastens the passing of a government in question, as suggested by Dulles, may be debatable. But there is hardly any doubt that the act of recognition is of considerable value to a new government. As T. C. Chen puts it:

> Recognition. . . is of great importance from the political, economic and psychological points of view. This importance should not be overlooked, still less ignored, but should be appreciated and given its proper weight in the decisions of States on the question of recognition.[34]

* * *

Another related issue where views differ widely is as to whether recognition should be granted to a state which tends to disregard its international obligations. Arthur H. Dean, who generally favors a modification of the American policy toward China, says:

> The United States has consistently required as a condition of recognition that a new foreign government be able and willing to fulfill the international obligations of the state which it purports to represent.[35]

In the case of Communist China, however, some critics of the official American position are inclined to compromise on this point and to take a position of forgiveness in a hope that it would stimulate the Chinese Communists to abide by the international standards of behavior in the future.[36]

14

Quincy Wright, along with some other writers on international law, tends to consider the actual record of behavior of a country irrelevant.[37]

The validity of this test is also questioned by T. C. Chen who says:

> This requirement [of fulfilling international obligations] has often been used as a pretext for withholding recognition whenever the wish of the recognizing State is not fully complied with. It is no longer a question of the fulfillment of obligations according to international law, but a question of the fulfillment of obligations according to the wish of the recognizing State.[38]

The argument, advanced by Barnett and some others that "the Peking regime doubtless passes this test [i.e., of carrying out its international obligations] in much the same way as the other Communist governments recognized by the United States"[39] is probably one of the strongest so far. After all, it is difficult to stand on a principle after numerous departures from it have already been made. Indeed, why shouldn't the United States recognize Communist China the same way it has recognized other communist countries? The Chinese Communists should not be much worse than the Russians, and the situation appears essentially similar. If we have compromised on our principles in the past, we might just as well go ahead and do the same in the case of China. This argument is usually countered by the answer that whenever recognition has been extended in the past to communist governments, it has never been done under the circumstances when such governments had been expressing implacable hostility toward the United States or were openly defiant of the rules of traditional international behavior. The Chinese Communist regime, declared Secretary Dulles, "is bitterly hateful of the United States which it considers a principal obstacle in the way of its path of conquest."[40] In the above quoted statement, the Department of State stresses the same point:

> The Chinese Communist regime has made no secret of its fundamental hostility to the United States and the free world nor of its avowed intention to effect their downfall.[41]

The Department of State has insisted on viewing the case of recognition of Communist China as very different from that of

Soviet Russia. Secretary Dulles, while not questioning recognition of the Soviet Union under the circumstances existing in 1933, expresses confidence that "that recognition would not have been accorded even in 1933 had there been clear warning that Soviet promises given in this connection were totally unreliable, that aggressive war would soon become an instrumentality of Soviet policy, and that it would be neutral toward Japanese aggression in Asia."[42]

In the case of Communist China, according to Secretary Dulles, the United States has been forewarned: that regime fails to pass even the tests the Soviet regime seemed to pass:

1. Soviet Russia, in 1933, had had a decade of peaceful and nonaggressive relations with neighboring states; Communist China's past record is one of armed aggression.
2. The Soviet regime seemed to want peace for the future. In the case of Communist China the situation is quite the reverse. . . .
3. The Soviet Union in 1933 was not flagrantly violating its international engagements. The Chinese Communist regime is violating the 1953 Korean armistice and the 1954 Indochina armistice.
4. There was reason to hope that the Soviet regime would treat our nationals with respect. The Chinese Communist regime violates the persons of our citizens in defiance of the elementary code of international decency, and it breaches its 1955 pledge to release them.
5. It seemed, in 1933, that the Soviet regime and the United States had parallel interests in resisting Japanese aggression in the Far East. Today the political purposes of Communist China clash everywhere with our own.[43]

Implicit in this statement is a feeling of regret that the United States recognized the Soviet Union. This underlines the fact that recognition, once extended, cannot be withdrawn — unless the subject country is involved in a war or a revolution and a rival government is set up. Under those conditions foreign governments sometimes hurry to recognize the rival regime despite the legal opinion that "premature recognition is a tortious act against the legal government [and] is a breach of international law."[44] This happens, of course, when intervention with the purpose of influencing the developments in a country torn by war is intended. It can be added that in recent times this form of intervention has been practiced almost exclusively by the communist governments.

So, as we have seen, in matters of international law and international morality, as related to the problem of recognition of Communist China, the critics and the defenders of the non-recognition policy occupy virtually irreconcilable positions. History, however, knows many instances when international law has been disregarded and when high principles have been sacrificed to the practical needs of the United States foreign policy. Secretary Dulles was repeatedly accused of a tendency to approach international problems in terms of "good" and "bad" and, as it was alleged, of excessive moralizing. Such an approach, however, has strong defenders. Professor Percy E. Corbett states unequivocally that "the view that foreign policy is a domain alien to morals is patently untenable."[45] This position is also emphasized by Hornbeck:

> The American policy is rooted in a belief in the reality of a corpus of natural, moral or divinely ordained law and a practical application of principles evolved and expounded in the corpus of Christian doctrine. . . . We must first, last and always be true to our own heritage of concepts, principles and commitments.[46]

At the same time we see that even Dulles himself believes the moral argument to be subsidiary to other considerations determining the position of the United States government:

> At any time it will serve the interests of the United States to recognize the Chinese Communist regime, we will do it. We are not controlled by dogma or anything of that sort. It's a very simple question: Will it serve our interests and the interests of the free world and our allies to whom we are commited to grant recognition? If the answer to that is that it will help it, then we will recognize. If the answer is that it will not help it, then we will not recognize, and the answer today is "no." [47]

Therefore, problems of morality aside, the United States has taken the position that recognition of Communist China could do this country no good. Secretary Dulles stated the case for the government:

> United States diplomatic recognition of the Chinese Communist regime would serve no national purpose but would strengthen and encourage influences hostile to us and our allies and further imperil lands whose independence is related to our peace and security.[48]

17

The Department of State added:

> Recognition would produce no tangible benefits to the United States or the free world as a whole and would be of material assistance to Chinese Communist attempts to extend Communist domination throughout Asia.[49]

Also, on the negative side, a guiding consideration remains that the Peking regime keeps reiterating its hostility towards the United States. The government has contended that to aid one's enemy is folly, and, as it has already been shown, recognition is of definite value to a government to which it is extended. The critics challenge this, insisting that the "importance of the recognition has been grossly exaggerated," but the supporters of the nonrecognition policy remain unimpressed. Hornbeck says:

> Diplomatic recognition has a value — especially to the state or government to which it is accorded. . . . [It] gives birth to a corpus of rights and duties. In theory these rights and duties are reciprocally identical. . . . but in practice the according state imposes upon itself obligations and confers upon the recipient rights without assurance that the latter will reciprocate. The consequences to the accorder may be either a gain or a loss, but to the recipient they can only be a gain.[50]

Thus, the legal arguments remain inconclusive. In all evidence, the question has to be resolved on political grounds. Since the "international law concerning recognition. . . [is] somewhat unsatisfactory on all essential points."[51]

CONSEQUENCES OF RECOGNITION

Since there is no compulsion, under international law, for the United States to recognize the Communist Government of China the case apparently has to be decided on other merits. What the policy of nonrecognition has produced so far is known. It is relatively easy to foresee what a continuation of this policy would produce in the near future. It is less easy to predict possible conse-

18

quences of a reversal of this policy, in terms of political and strategic gains and losses to the United States.

As it is to be expected, the estimates of these consequences by the critics of nonrecognition substantially differ from those of its defenders. Nevertheless, since both sides accept certain basic premises, their disagreement is more that of degree and the debate preserves rational forms.

Before we proceed with specific arguments, it might be advisable to clarify the qualitative difference in the position of both sides, which remains implicit in their approach to the problem. The critics draw their inspiration from the visible abnormality of a situation in which a *de facto* government of a nation of more than 600 million people has been excluded, almost entirely, from the formal diplomatic activities of the United States. They are also extremely sensitive to foreign criticism of the American position, especially to that coming from certain circles in the "neutralist" countries and from some Western countries. On the whole, they refuse to share the government's view that "recognition would produce no tangible benefits" and feel that they can point out at least some such benefits. Still, we notice that once the controversy moves into the field of practical politics, the critics find themselves largely on the defensive.

This phenomenon cannot be understood unless we appreciate the basic distinction between a policy-maker and an outsider who disagrees with a certain policy, even an outsider in perfect command of pertaining facts.[52]

It is this difference in approach which leaves the critics of the official policy on rather shaky ground. The pivotal fact remains that the government bears ultimate responsibility for the nation's well being and is a legitimate interpreter of what is good and what is bad for the country. While the decision-makers are mortals and may err in judgment, it has to be assumed that they have in their possession more information than is available to individual scholars, journalists, and politicians. They have to weigh this data against a broad variety of constantly changing considerations which may not occur to, or which may be underestimated or ignored altogether by, the critics of a particular aspect of policy. The inertia characterizing government operations may be due, in part, to the usual inflexibility of bureaucracy. On the other hand, the government is acutely aware of the interdependence of many and varied aspects of policy and naturally tries to avoid any earthshaking changes which may upset the whole structure of its relations with the outside world. It also has to be conscious of the trends in domestic public opinion as manifested in the press, and particularly in Congress. One valid factor in the American China policy has been the fact that since 1951, Congress has repeatedly declared, almost unanimously, its uncompromising opposition to recognition of Communist China and/or its seating in the United Nations.[53] To quote one representative albeit "controversial" opinion:

> Common sense provides its own answer: we cannot recognize Red China, since she is defiant of her crimes against her own people and indeed of all humanity, unrepentent of the terrors she has already unleashed, and determined to continue her campaign of terror beyond her own borders whenever possible. To recognize her would be a cynical surrender of America's position as champion of the oppressed peoples in both Europe and Asia.[54]

Once congressional opposition is put in such unequivocal form, it becomes something few Presidents can disregard, especially in view of certain constitutional rights of the Senate in the conduct of foreign affairs.

All this explains why the critics of nonrecognition find themselves under an obvious disadvantage. Whatever their arguments be, they are based largely on speculation, for no one can guarantee that, on balance, a radical change of policy toward Communist China would result in tangible benefits to the United States. Moreover, at least some of them are painfully aware that such a change is likely to be paid for by substantial damage to the defense posture of the United States and its strategic position *vis-a-vis* the communist bloc. This point is indicated by Pitman B. Potter:

> Obviously the most compelling considerations for the United States are the possible military value of the control of Formosa and the Strait by or in the name of Chiang Kai-shek and the fact that the Communists do dominate continental China. Reconciling these two considerations is evidently not easy or simple and it is just possible that no reconciliation of these two viewpoints is possible.[55]

*   *   *

20

Even the most outspoken critics of the official policy, even those who tend to take a cynical view of treaty obligations and loyalty to one's allies, do not challenge the assumption that to have Taiwan in friendly hands is indispensable for the defense of the United States. And since by tradition, politics are expected to stop at the water's edge, there are few critics who are willing to take the blame for weakening America's position in the world. So long as all of them agree that recognition of Communist China and/or its seating in the United Nations would undermine the Nationalists' hold on Taiwan, they are compelled to proceed with caution.[56]

Thus the so-called Conlon Report, recently published by the Senate Foreign Relations Committee, while arguing that we should not maintain the fiction that Chiang's government represents China, concedes:

> Certainly the admission of Communist China [to the United Nations] would be a heavy blow at the National Government.[57]

However, the Conlon Report is possibly the only recent document which suggests — without taking credit for the suggestion — that destruction of the Nationalist would not necessarily hurt American interests:

> Continued recognition of the Nationalist Government as that of China seems most unpromising. . . . The acceptance of Taiwan as a part of mainland China? This alone would satisfy the Chinese Communists at present, and therefore remove what is otherwise likely to be a continuing source of trouble. Indeed, it has been argued that Taiwan is not so important from a military or political viewpoint as to warrant *ipso facto* the enormous risk of a long-term United States commitment for its defense. It has even been suggested that a general settlement in Asia might be attempted whereby Taiwan would be united with the mainland in exchange for a Communist agreement to accept free elections under United Nations auspices throughout Korea, leading to the unification of that country.[58]

This statement deserves some extra attention. To begin with, the United States government assumes that any agreement with the communists is not worth much unless it is self-enforcing. Then there is a question of agreement on exact meaning of what constitutes "free elections," for differences of definition can be decisive.

21

On March 8, 1961, *Pravda* reported that the North Korean government issued a memorandum demanding "free elections" in Korea — but on condition of prior withdrawal of the American troops from South Korea and dissolution of the United Nations Commission for the Unification and Rehabilitation of Korea which, it was alleged, "serves as a tool of the aggressive policies of the United States." But even if there were a chance for a truly free election — in the Western sense of the word — and for a unification of Korea, it is doubtful whether the United States would be willing to pay for it by abandoning Taiwan, for the government takes the position that

> Formosa is a vital link in the free world's island chain of defenses in the Pacific. . . . If Formosa should fall to the Communists, Japan, the Philippines, and all of Southeast Asia would be seriously threatened.[59]

Guided by the same considerations, the government has further contended that "recognition of Communist China by the United States would seriously cripple, if not destroy altogether, the Government of the Republic of China,"[60] and Secretary Dulles, with characteristic moral overtones, adds that "we are honorbound to give our ally, to whom we are pledged by a mutual defense treaty, a full measure of loyalty."[61]

Some may view a loyalty to one's allies as a rather old-fashioned virtue. There are scholars and politicians who would consider backing out of a treaty or letting an ally fall if this would help to remove some of the obstacles to an attainment of a desirable national goal. In practice, however, the United States has avoided such actions and maybe not so much for ethical and moral considerations but because the international commitments represent such a complex structure of interdependent relationships with the outside world that any frivolity with treaty obligations endangers more than it solves. To allow the communists to take over Taiwan in an unrealistic hope that this might turn the Peking regime into a relaxed, nonaggressive power is something more than the United States has been prepared to do.

But if the United States is resolved to protect Taiwan from the communist "liberation" it automatically commits itself — from Peking's point of view — to a posture implacably hostile to the communist regime of China, regardless of true feelings in Wash-

22

ington. As a result, the positions freeze and an establishment of normal relations between the two countries becomes impossible. This, however, does not impress the critics of nonrecognition not hamstrung by responsibilities involved in directing the country's foreign policy.

The government has pointed out that recognition, besides threatening the Nationalists' hold on Taiwan, would be a blow to all anti-communists on the mainland.

Barnett speculates that "it is doubtful that American non-recognition contributes positively to the growth of an anti-Communist movement on the mainland of China or increases the chances that an effective opposition to the Peking regime will emerge."[62] Such contentions, however, seem to be debatable. American non-recognition may not contribute substantially to *the growth* of resistance on the China mainland. But recognition, if granted, is bound to undermine *the very existence* of resistance there. As to the possible soothing effect of recognition on Peking's violent anti-Americanism, this appears strictly speculative. Some defenders of the official policy insist that the United States cannot afford to make any friendly gestures. Rowe says:

> The West, and particularly the United States cannot relax its hostility toward the Chinese Communist regime by concessions in either economic or political fields; . . . . our support of the Republic of China on Taiwan must be used as a positive weapon of political warfare against Communist China.[63]

Professor Paul K. T. Sih sees the effects of recognition as going far beyond the Far East:

> Should we recognize Red China, the cause of resistance to Communism would suffer everywhere, and both the survival of Chinese Communism and its further aggression would be assured.[64]

*   *   *

The United States views the fate of Taiwan as closely linked to that of other countries of the Far East:

> If the United States were to abandon the Republic of China in order to placate the insatiable Red Chinese, no

23

country in Asia could feel that they could any longer rely on the protection of the United States against the Communist threat.[65]

Present United States policies in that area are determined by its strategic needs, by bilateral treaties with Korea, Japan and the Chinese Nationalist government on Taiwan, and by regional defense alliances, SEATO and ANZUS. These treaties and alliances the Peking regime considers not only hostile to itself but also inimical to the nations participating in them:

> If the U.S. Government agreed to withdraw its troops from Asian countries and to liquidate its military bases there, friendship between the people of the United States and these Asian countries could be developed, and, moreover, the possibility would arise of realizing peaceful coexistence between the U.S. Government and these Asian countries.[66]

The American view has been that these alliances are strictly defensive and that they have been brought about by the aggressiveness of the Chinese Communists themselves. Assistant Secretary of State for Far Eastern Affairs, J. Graham Parsons, said:

> It is sometimes argued that our policy is provocative to Communist China. Actually, the exact reverse is true. Our collective security structure was developed only *after* unprovoked Communist agression against Korea. Our Mutual Defense treaty with the Republic of China was drawn up only *after* Communist China's attacks on Quemoy in 1954. SEATO came into being only *after* the fall of Dien Bien Phu, when Communist armies were threatening to overrun all of Southeast Asia.[67]

And a year later, Tillman Durdin wrote in the *New York Times* on March 12, 1961:

> Communist China's ultimate aim is clearly to be the dominant power in Asia — an Asia that Peiping intends to see embrace communism. For the present, at least, the Chinese Communists are pushing toward this objective by means of subversive agents, by propaganda, by the support in some countries of Communist and pro-Communist insurgents and by continuously seeking to turn Asians against the United States. . . . In the circumstances, United States policy has had to be based on the maintenance of armed

24

strength, the continuance of support to our Asian allies and persistence in efforts to convince the people of Asia that friendship with the United States and resistance to communism offer a better future than succumbing to the Communists.

A communique issued by President Kennedy and the Prime Minister of New Zealand, Keith J. Holyoake, on March 3, 1961, "noted with deep concern the hostile and aggressive attitude of the Chinese Communist regime and the particular menace it poses to the peace of Asia, Africa and Latin America." It also stressed "the importance and value of SEATO and ANZUS."[68]

The situation in Southeast Asia is dominated by the fact that half a dozen nations, some of which have never had very strong governments, live under the ever-present shadow of Communist China. Even when there is no overt aggression on the part of the communists, the mere proximity of Communist China generates significant internal presures. Nonrecognition of Communist China — only in part inspired by the American example — has been one of the means the local governments employ for their self-protection.[69]

People who like to be cynical about it, often ask whether these governments are viable anyway and worth supporting. The consensus of experts, however, seems to be that if relieved from outside threats they could continue on indefinitely, either as pro-Western, or as neutral. Since, however, the threat *is* there, a question should be posed whether American backing can produce sufficient counterbalance to the communist pressure. For the time being, at least, the United States appears determined to carry out its obligations in that region. President Kennedy said:

> [The Chinese Communists] have been, as we know, extremely belligerent towards us and they've been unfailing in their attacks upon the United States. . . . [In part, this has been] because they recognize that the United States is committed. . . to maintaining its connections with other countries and committed to its own defense and the defense of freedom. . . . I would like to see a lessening of that tension. But we are not prepared to surrender in order to get a relaxation of tension.[70]

An unwillingness of the United States to "surrender" is interpreted by some Asian neutralists as manifestation of American belligerence and unreasonableness. Certain American critics of the government, who hold in particular esteem the views of such leaders as Nehru and Sukarno, insist that as a result of recognition "the general American posture in Asia would be improved in their eyes," that "far from being disastrous, a change of American policy toward China might actually open up new opportunities for strengthening the non-Communist position in Asia."[71]

The opponents of recognition take exception to such views. Richard L. Walker states emphatically:

> The opinion. . . advanced by irresponsible intellectuals and some leaders in the neutralist camp that the United States is a threat to peace, is nothing but fraud when advanced as "Asian opinion." Surely in the Far East this view is not shared by the leaders among the Koreans, free Chinese, Vietnamese, Filipinos, Thais or Malayans. It is doubtful whether it is chared by a large number of spokesmen among the Iranians, Iraquis, Turks or Pakistanis.[73]

And, concludes Walker,

> What it means, therefore, is that change in our China policy is advocated in terms of pleasing neutralist leaders who presume to speak for Asia and with the faint hope of persuading them, at the expense of our allies in Asia, that somehow we are not as bad as they say.[73]

An interesting suggestion on the subject of "Asian opinion" comes from the authors of the Conlon Report (and some other writers), who question the sincerity of neutralist leaders:

> In spite of a public stand in favor of Chinese Communist trade, cultural relations, recognition, or United Nations membership, some of the [neutralist] governments are secretly happy with the current American position.[74]

This position was reaffirmed by Vice-President Johnson upon the completion of his tour of Asia in a joint communique issued with Chiang Kai-shek on May 15, 1961:

> The Vice-President, on behalf of President Kennedy, assured President Chiang that: the United States means to stand with her allies in the Asian area; the United States has no intention of recognizing the Peiping regime; the United States opposes seating the Peiping regime in the

United Nations and regards it as important that the position of the Republic of China in the United Nations should be maintained.

* * *

The concern of the Western-oriented countries of the Far East appears to be twofold. On the one hand, there is apprehension over direct pressure — military, economic, political, cultural — emanating from China. This danger, presumably, is counterbalanced by economic aid and military backing from the United States and by the cultural interchange with the West. On the other hand, there is a fear of subversion and guerilla warfare directed and supported by the Soviet and Chinese Communists, against which the alliance with the United States provides little remedy — as the Laotian episode has amply indicated. Linked with the threat of subversion is the problem of large Chinese minorities which for centuries have been living in the countries on the fringes of China, unable and unwilling to assimilate with the native population. The political orientation of these "overseas Chinese" has been a major factor in the domestic situation of these countries.

The advocates of revision of United States policy believe that the fears of subversion directed from Communist China have been exaggerated. The authors of the Conlon Report say that "there is considerable evidence that indigenous Communist movements in South and Southeast Asia got little Chinese assistance."[75] As to the over twelve million overseas Chinese, according to the same source, the Mao Tse-tung government avoids supporting them, not wanting to alienate the governments which are either neutralist, or leaning towards closer relations with Communist China.

A. Doak Barnett considers the developments among the overseas Chinese to be of marginal significance. He believes, that even if their loyalties were to switch from Taiwan to Peking, this would not present a major political threat — except in Singapore, Malaya and Thailand. At any rate, says Barnett, the "American policy of nonrecognition has little bearing on the causes of this danger." This, however, does not prevent him from recommending (just in case) that

Until the governments of Singapore, Malaya, and Thailand achieve a greater degree of political stability. . . they

27

would be well advised to continue limiting their contacts with Peking and refraining from establishing formal diplomatic relations with Communist China.[76]

Philip E. Mosely views the shift of allegiances among the overseas Chinese as inevitable:

As Communist China has grown in political and military strength, the national pride of the overseas Chinese and their resentment of the inferior position to which they have generally been relegated by the nations among which they reside, have tended to focus their loyalties on mainland China, now admired as a major power.[77]

A similar opinion is expressed by the authors of the Conlon Report, who believe that the overseas Chinese "would have to pay some homage to Communist China," and who think that "Taiwan can never be a satisfactory symbol for the China mainland"; that is, for those of the Chinese who are in opposition to the communist regime.

Despite such pessimistic views, the State Department refuses to consider the situation hopeless and to concede the overseas Chinese to the Communists without a fight. And it ties United States policy to the issue:

The Nationalist government is a symbol, the only rallying point in the world. . . — the only alternative to communism for millions of Chinese on the mainland and throughout Southeast Asia. If the Nationalist government should be liquidated, some 12 million overseas Chinese would automatically become citizens of Red China and potential cells of infiltration and subversion against the governments of the countries where they reside.[78]

This position is supported by Thomas K. Finletter who says that

A recognition of Peking by the United States and the United Nations would undoubtedly help the mainland communists in their efforts to manipulate the overseas Chinese and to swing them to the communist cause.[79]

The opponents of recognition point out that an increasing number of young Chinese from overseas settlements go to study in Taiwan universities (over 6,000 in 1958-59) rather than to mainland China — although this is explained by some experts to be a result

28

of a much tougher screening of the candidates by Peking. Yet, it cannot be denied that at least to some extent the traditional cultural pattern of the Chinese people works in favor of the overseas Chinese pro-Nationalist stand. While it may well be true, as indicated by Mosely, that many of them do look to Communist China for protection against discrimination in the countries where they reside, the trend is not universal. For example, the Chinese appeals for help against discriminatory policies of the Sukarno government in 1960 were directed to *both* Mao Tse-tung and Chiang Kai-shek. Continuing American nonrecognition may not affect the situation appreciably; on the other hand, the recognition of the Peking regime would obviously let down the still significant — if not predominant — group of those who politically and emotionally are on the side of the Nationalists. In some countries of the Far East their shift might be decisive and spell the difference between a pro-Western and a pro-Communist orientation. To "discourage" Singapore, Thailand, or Malaya from following American recognition of Communist China, as suggested by Barnett, would be far easier said than done.

Thus we see the pattern of thinking behind current United States policy toward China emerging with reasonable clarity. There is an awareness that recognition of the Chinese Communist government is apt to lead to abandoning the Nationalists on Taiwan; that the Nationalists would be unable to withstand the subsequent pressure from the communist-dominated mainland on their own and, deprived of unqualified American support, would collapse. Besides endangering the chain of American defenses in the Pacific, the downfall of the Nationalist government would be likely to lead to political shifts in Far Eastern nations which, in turn, would produce there either communist or, at the very best, anti-American-oriented regimes. So far, the United States has refrained from any move which could bring about or facilitate this presumed development.

* * *

As if aware that the demand for a "truly realistic" approach to the China problem is not sufficiently convincing by itself, the critics bring into the discussion arguments of manifestly minor importance. One such argument is that of the value of continuous contact. Barnett says:

> Many non-Communist nations, and at least some American critics of present United States policy toward China, believe that there can be definite advantages in maintaining continuous diplomatic contacts even with the governments clearly hostile. . . especially with those nations which, like Communist China, pose the greatest problems for American policy.[80]

The Department of State does not challenge such contentions openly: after all, the United States *is* maintaining sizeable embassies throughout the communist world. But those who are not restrained by their official position are quick to point out that the advantages of keeping "listening posts" in the enemy camp are, to say the least modest. They stress that Peking is probably the worst place for Western diplomats to be stationed and they illustrate the point by listing endless indignities and strictures on normal diplomatic function suffered there by Great Britain, which had recognized the communist regime from the outset. They also cite the experiences of Western journalists in China who, whenever they are in need of general information about the country, have to make trips to Hong Kong or Tokyo. And, as many an American diplomat with experience in a communist country would affirm, there is little that could be done in a communist capital in the way of listening that could not be done with about the same success in a good library back home. In its editorial on November 20, 1959, the *New York Times* said:

> The hostility between Communist China and the West is reflected in the faces and in the behavior of Western diplomats in Peiping. On the whole, the envoys of the West seem to be unhappy, frustrated men. They have virtually no contact with the people who matter in Peiping. They get little information about what is going on within China. They are starved of reliable statistics and facts. . . . The hate of Peiping toward the West creates a barrier through which no Western diplomats can pass.

Another marginal argument in favor of recognition deals with trade and cultural relations with Communist China. At present the United States has a total embargo on trade with Peking which it

30

established following the United Nations General Assembly resolution in April 1951. It has also tried (for the most part unsuccessfully) to influence its allies to restrict their trade with the Chinese Communists. The critics of the United States policy contend that this situation ought to be changed, that trade and cultural relations, once established, would pave the way to the creation of a spirit of good will between the two countries.

This contention appears to be of little substance in view of the experience of other Western countries which trade with Communist China. The communist regimes, although anxious to import certain machinery and equipment, have consistently avoided a situation when their economies might become dependent on trade with the "capitalist" countries. At times, trade was used as an attraction in order to influence business circles or governments in the West but, as the United States points out,

> Such trade would always be at the mercy of Communist policies. Peiping uses trade as means of exerting pressure on the trading partner whenever it deems this to be expedient.[81]

In addition, the government insists there is no reason to think that "trade is dependent on recognition." Many Western countries have been trading with the Chinese Communists on a large scale without extending diplomatic recognition to Peking. As to Sino-American trade,

> The United States, which has heavy security commitments in the China area, ought not build up the military power of its potential enemy. We also doubt the value of cultural relations.[82]

Barnett agrees that "recognition is not an absolute prerequisite to dealing with Communist China"[83] and, for this reason, does not attach too much importance to the pleas for expanding trade or establishing "listening posts." To him, recognition is primarily a political act and a way to improve the atmosphere on the Far East in general and to achieve a change of heart among the communist leadership. He also speculates that

> Possibly the United States' policy of nonrecognition is itself a factor reinforcing the Chinese Communists' inclination to be unyielding and recalcitrant.[84]

31

Barnett's other suggestion is that, in a way, the American position makes it easier for Peking to achieve its internal goals:

> It is possible. . . that the United States present posture toward China actually makes it easier. . . for Peking to mobilize active support for its anti-American policies.[85]

It is easy to see that there is a contradiction implicit in the two statements. Is the Peking government merely inclined to be "unyielding and recalcitrant"? Or is it actually happy over the American "present posture" which allows it to "mobilize active support" of the mainland Chinese for its policies? If the former is correct, a case conceivably could be made for modification of the American policy in hope that this would favorably affect the communists' natural inclinations. If the latter is correct, however, an attempt to produce a friendly attitude in Peking by the act of recognition and some other ouvertures would obviously be futile. The Peking leaders themselves make no secret that such is the case.[86]

Should the United States consider additional concessions? On this subject there are two schools of thought. One believes that the West must accommodate the communists if we are to secure peace and build a decent world community. Another school points out the past record of dealing with dictatorships bent on aggression and insists that concessions are likely to lead to disaster:

> It always seems tempting to many men of good-will in the West to try to disprove. . . the Communist analysis and to alleviate east-west tensions by advancing as far as possible toward the satisfaction of the interests and demands of the Communists. Yet it is doubtful whether any such policy would work with the Communists better than with Hitler.[87]

There is something to this, for it is difficult to imagine that concessions on the part of the West will not encourage the ambitions of the Chinese Communists in what they consider to be their mission of spreading communism in Asia. It is up to the United States government to evaluate such a possibility, for vastly more is involved here than a mere embarrassment of extending so much delayed diplomatic recognition to Communist China.

Without prejudging the case, however, let us look at another set of arguments which appear quite strong on their face but which have little direct relation to the possible developments in the Far East.

RECOGNITION AND DISARMAMENT

The argument that recognition of Communist China is imperative if the nuclear test ban and general disarmament are to be hoped
for is often being used out of the context of the direct Sino-American
relations and, because of it, deserves to be treated separately.

The necessity of making Communist China a part of the future
international arms-control and disarmament agreements is obvious
— at least if one is to assume that such agreements are forthcoming.
A case for recognition of the Peking regime by the United States
(and its admission to the United Nations), as a precondition for
negotiations on these issues, appears strong on the face of it. To
object to a step which might help to bring about disarmament in
our nuclear age and to assure "peace for our generation" is equal to
coming out against motherhood and for sin. It is self-evident that
if disarmament agreements are to be effective, Communist China
has to participate in them — a point made by Chou En-lai himself:

> It goes without saying that any disarmament agreement
> would not be binding on China if it was reached without the
> participation of, and was not signed by, the official Chinese
> representative. This we have declared on many occasions.[88]

But is this only a question of formal participation in negotiations? Would a mere recognition of the Chinese Communists' right
to be admitted as equals to a conference table make them more
amenable? Thomas E. Murray, who has been critical of the American
policy on unilateral cessation of nuclear tests, shows how political
problems and the necessity to assure effective inspection interlock
in this field:

> An inspection system devised largely at the insistence of
> the United States will not be accepted by a country which
> the United States, for many complex reasons, refuses to
> recognize and which is, if anything, even more bellicose
> than the USSR. The nuclear test issue is not an argument
> for suddenly reversing U.S. policy toward China. But the

China problem *is* in itself a sufficient reason for the United States to reverse its nuclear test policy.[89]

Chester Bowles suggests the opposite, namely that it is the United States policy toward China that needs to be changed:

> A realistic approach to disarmament must consider the interests and ambitions of the swaggering Communist government in Peking. We cannot indefinitely disregard the presence on this planet of 650 million of militant Chinese, whose leaders, in the absence of some enforceable agreement, will sooner or later possess nuclear weapons.[90]

A. Doak Barnett lists the reasons why a militarily strong Communist China would be of particular danger:

> Communist China is at present a frustrated nation, and the combination of great ambitions, growing power, and deep frustration can be a dangerous mixture. . . . It has significant unsatisfied claims to territories that it promises to 'liberate', by military force if necessary. . . . It is also the only major power that is excluded from the most important international councils.[91]

Having said this, however, Barnett mutes part of the alarm by stating that the Chinese Communists "are by no means wholly rigid or reckless; they are, in fact, capable of calculated self-control and restraint." Still, Barnett believes that Peking has a very strong bargaining position because of the world clamor for disarmament. The first step for the West is "to insure Communist Chinese participation. The question is not whether Communist China should be included, but rather how and when." Full-fledged participation in disarmament talks, according to Barnett, would be only a part of the price the Chinese Communists would demand in return for their consent to sit down and negotiate. They are also likely to demand membership in the United Nations, recognition of their territorial claims to the off-shore islands and Taiwan, and maybe even the withdrawal of American nuclear power from Asia. "They could bargain by merely doing nothing — by being obstructionist — in the hope that the pressure of world opinion might ultimately impel the Western powers to make concessions."[92]

Barnett does not say whether the Chinese Communists are likely to stop "being obstructionist" in case they got what they bargained for. Aside from some vague hints, they so far have avoided committing themselves to any scheme of disarmament and inspection which has been advanced by the present members of the Atomic Club; they have not voiced their support even for the schemes proposed by the Soviet Union. In fact, it has been repeatedly reported that the Peking leadership takes a rather dim view of the Soviet professed willingness to discuss peace with the West, and that Mao's dictum that "political power grows out of the barrel of a gun" is still in effect in China.

The question, how to induce Communist China or, for that matter, any other Nth country with a nuclear power potential to participate in a disarmament and arms-control agreement, has not been answered by anyone. Kissinger views the outlook skeptically:

> It is important to remember that no Nth country so far has indicated any willingness to join the agreement. France, indeed, has explicitly refused. It will be no easy matter to negotiate an elaborate inspection system for Communist China — especially since it is hard to see what Communist China would gain in return for such an agreement when we have already stopped testing.[93]

James E. Dougherty voices the same doubts and points out the core of the problem:

> No one has yet come forth with a politically satisfactory explanation of just how the "Big Three" solution is to be imposed upon all the other nations of the world, especially those with nuclear-power ambitions (France and Red China). . . . It is very doubtful that either the French or Chinese Communist leadership will be deterred from developing their own nuclear arsenal. . . The futility of the disarmament effort was but a symptom of a much more profound malaise — the *political* failure to resolve the conflict of national interests.[94]

That the absence of the political settlement between the warring sides represents a major stumbling block in any disarmament negotiations is indicated also by Hans J. Morgenthau,[95] and George Kennan.[96]

Emery Reves offers this observation:

> If we want to discuss seriously the problem of peace in this magnificent and highly dangerous age of nuclear fission

and fusion, we must first realize that our thinking and our action are threatened by two fallacies: The first fallacy is that we can secure peace by armament. And the second fallacy is that we can secure peace by disarmament. Endless historical evidence proves the incontrovertible fact that peace is not a technical problem, not a military problem, but essentially a political and social problem.[97]

Once we assume that any disarmament must be preceded by a political settlement we begin to see in its true light the relation of recognition to disarmament. It is obvious that no political settlement is possible until normal diplomatic relations are established between Washington and Peking. It is equally obvious that the existence of diplomatic relations is no guarantee that such political settlement can be achieved, as the whole history of Soviet-American relations illustrates. The argument is that a first step should be made in that direction nevertheless, and that recognition of Communist China should be the first step. In order to have this step made successfuly, however, it is imperative that the Peking regime *accept* American recognition. The question is, will it? Barnett has shown a price tag which Peking is likely to put for its agreement to negotiate with the West. Chester Bowles indicates Peking's likely reaction to American recognition:

> If we should propose an exchange of ambassadors, Mao Tse-tung would surely ask if our recognition extended to Communist sovereignty over "the Province of Formosa". And when we replied that it did not, his response would inevitably be a contemptuous refusal of our offer.[98]

Since, in Mr. Bowles' words, "a realistic approach to disarmament must consider the interests and ambitions of the swaggering Communist government in Peking,"[99] the implication is clear that recognition of communist sovereignty over "the Province of Formosa" must be a part of a "realistic approach to disarmament."

This was fully appreciated throughout the years of the Eisenhower administration which was not willing to plot a "handover" of Taiwan in possible return for a consent on the part of the Chinese Communists to accept recognition. However, being aware of international pressures for disarmament, the government had to take a cautious position. Secretary Herter, pointing out that the talks, even with the Soviets alone, have not so far yielded any

36

positive results, doubted "the necessity of bringing Red China in until the nations that are going to be sitting at the conference table come nearer to the agreement." Herter also took the position that negotiating with Peking, when and if that stage is reached, "would not necessarily require Chinese Communist membership in the United Nations any more than it would require recognition by any power of China."[100]

The pressures on the government "to do something" about disarmament are great and are likely to continue to grow. This may result in hasty and premature steps which would be regretted later. China is not a nuclear power yet and according to Professor Oskar Morgenstern,

> will not be a superpower for a long time to come. This time of transition is crucial for the world and exceedingly dangerous. . . . It is the time when the present big powers should try to stop the newcomer from becoming big and aligning himself with the big opponent.[101]

At the same time, Morgenstern sounds a note of warning:

> It would be foolish to initiate the cooperative course without having made sure that cooperation will actually take place. The mere fact that we find the cooperative case intellectually so much more attractive and that it is clearly in the interests of world peace should not induce us to choose cooperation if the other side shows no understanding and does not choose it also. It takes at least two to cooperate.[102]

This puts a strong check on any far-reaching moves of the United States toward meeting communist desires. A desire to disarm must exist on the other side and must manifest itself in definite form before there is a hope for success. This desire cannot be produced by any well-meant gestures such as recognition. Yet, it is likely that if and when the United States decides to reverse its China policy it would use this pretext to justify not only recognition but other concessions as well.[103] Given the existing American feeling on the subject, the government would have to virtually succumb to fears of nuclear war if it were to decide to force the public and the Congress to acquiesce to recognition and to all other changes in the United States foreign policy which this step would inevitably bring about.

37

WHO SHOULD REPRESENT CHINA IN THE
UNITED NATIONS?

There is the argument that, regardless of what the United States is going to do about extending diplomatic recognition to Communist China, it should not oppose — in fact, it should promote — the seating of Mao Tse-tung's representatives in the United Nations. As one promoter of the idea of general accommodation with the Soviets puts it,

> we — not Russia — should propose before the General Assembly that Communist China be admitted to membership in the United Nations, to sit alongside Nationalist China in the General Assembly. . . . Our proposal to seat Communist China should be coupled with our recognition of Peking.[104]

Not every critic of the American China policy goes that far. But a substantial body of the champions of the "United Nations point of view" argues that for the good of the world organization Communist China must become a full-fledged member of it. This contention deserves serious consideration and we will return to it in the second part of this book. Now it woul be sufficient to state that not everything that is deemed good for the United Nations is necessarily good for the United States. Quite to the contrary, the Eisenhower administration held that the policy of nonrecognition is inextricably linked to its opposition to the Chinese Communist representation in the United Nations:

> Recognition of Peiping by the United States would inevitably lead to the seating of Peiping (in the United Nations). In view of the United States this would vitiate, if not destroy, the United Nations as an instrument for the maintenance of international peace.[105]

Such a strong opposition to the admission of Communist China to the United Nations has doubtless been dictated by a number of compelling considerations of which a desire to keep the United

Nations as an instrument of Western power has been but one. For instance, an opinion has been voiced by some legal authorities that admission to the United Nations of a new government automatically imposes on its members certain obligations toward such a government.[106] While this opinion — as most legal opinions on the United Nations members' obligations — is subject to interpretation, the implication is obvious: once Communist China is seated in that organization, there would be so much less that the United States would be able to do in a way of checking the spread of its power in Asia. At the same time, the government would be under pressure to take the next step and formally recognize the Peking regime. Whelan says:

> Admission of China to the U.N. with United States approval would undoubtedly be regarded as a *demarche* of the first importance, possibly even a prelude to formal recognition.[107]

The leaders of the Peking regime have displayed limited interest in membership in the United Nations. Consistently following their line they make their consent to join the world organization conditional. Chou En-lai recently said:

> China . . . will not participate in any meeting and organization in which the Chiang Kai-shek clique is included.[108]

In other words, the Republic of China would have to be thrown out of the United Nations before the Central People's Government of the People's Republic of China would agree to take its "rightful place" in that organization. There is a theoretical possibility that Chiang Kai-shek's representative could be unseated in the General Assembly by a two-thirds majority. There is no such possibility in the Security Council where the United States has a right of veto, that is if the government chooses to exercise this right. The critics of the American China policy have warned not to do it because this "would risk seriously straining or splitting the organization and would almost certainly have divisive effects tending to weaken rather than strengthen the entire non-Communist position."[109] Yet, in the past, it was repeatedly stated that the United States would resort to veto in order to prevent a Peking representative from occupying the permanent seat of China in the Security Council.

With the advent of the new administration in Washington, there have been signs suggesting that the issue of recognition might be divorced from that of Chinese representation in the United Nations. Such a divorce, however, promises to be a difficult trick to perform: an integrated foreign policy cannot allow for such contradictions in treatment of what has become a major problem, with the nation's interests so heavily dependent on its solution. We will return to this subject later on.

THE PRICE FOR RECOGNITION

Having reviewed the arguments for and against recognition of Communist China, let us take a look at the alternative to the present United States policy toward China. As would be expected, such an alternative is recognition of the Peking regime as a legitimate government of China, the exchange of ambassadors between Washington and Peking, and all other consequences which normally follow the act of diplomatic recognition.

This course, however, is not simple, and for two main reasons. One is that neither side is sufficiently anxious to establish direct relations. Another is that both sides regard recognition not as a first step towards the settlement of the disputes which divide them but, rather, as an act which must follow such a settlement. This means that negotiations must *precede* and *not follow* mutual recognition. At first glance, this still offers some room for hope, since both sides have declared, on many occasions, their willingness to negotiate.

A closer look, however, reveals a fundamental difference between the two sides in their approach to negotiations, and, more important, a question as to which issues are negotiable. The position for Communist China is stated by Chou En-lai:

Agreement must first be reached on matters of principle. When agreement on matters of principle cannot be reached, discussions on concrete matters are very difficult. Americans have the idea that when agreement cannot be reached on matters of principle, it is still good to seek, first, settlements on concrete matters. We tried this kind of approach in the early stage of the talks between China and the United States, namely, to lead to an agreement on major issues by settling first some concrete issues. But after trying it for many years, this approach proved unfeasible.[110]

What is this agreement "on matters of principle" that the Chinese Communist government is looking for? Chou En-lai provides the answer with remarkable clarity:

The two points of principle on which agreement should be reached are: 1) All disputes between China and the United States, including the dispute between the two countries in the Taiwan region, should be settled through peaceful negotiations, without resorting to the use or threat of force; and 2) the United States must agree to withdraw its armed forces from Taiwan and the Taiwan Straits.[111]

To clarify his position further, Chou En-lai says:

We hold that the dispute between China and the United States in the Taiwan region is an international question; whereas military action between the Central Government of New China and the Chiang Kai-shek clique in Taiwan is an internal question.[112]

And he states his position in such a way that there is no room for misunderstanding:

It is inconceivable that there can be diplomatic relations between China and the United States without a settlement of the dispute between the two countries in the Taiwan region.[113]

In other words, Peking is not going to accept American recognition or negotiate any other issue, unless and until the United States recognizes Peking's sovereignty over Taiwan, withdraws U.S. naval forces from the Taiwan Straits and evacuates whatever personnel, including its ambassador, it has on Taiwan itself.

The American position has been just as clear: the United States, for reasons it considers vital, continues to recognize the Chiang Kai-shek government on Taiwan as the legitimate government of China. As a concession to Peking — and to the realities of life —

the United States is willing to make sure that the Nationalists no longer represent a threat to the communist regime on the mainland — that is, a military threat. At the same time, it keeps reiterating its hope that someday, somehow, the communist regime in China will pass, and declares its intention to go to considerable lengths to accelerate that passing. In the meantime, it takes measures, in the form of a series of defensive alliances, aimed at "containing" Communist China in Asia.

The United States government does not see —or did not see until recently — any serious contradiction between its essentially hostile position towards Communist China and its efforts to lessen the tensions in the Far East. It has been willing, even anxious, to negotiate with Peking on certain "concrete issues," hoping that such negotiations might lead to some sort of *modus vivendi* with the Peking regime. These hopes were doomed for two reasons. The first reason is, that the "concrete issues" in which the United States has been interested (e.g., the release of American citizens held in captivity in China, questions dealing with policing of the Korean and Indochina armistices, exchanges of newspaper correspondents, etc.) have been of little, if any, interest to the Chinese Communists. The second is that while talking — quite sincerely — about its desire to alleviate tensions in the Far East, the United States has had in mind the relaxation of *its own* tensions, which happen to be different from those of the Peking government. In fact, given the general context of the global struggle between the two political systems, the tensions to which the United States has been subjected could be relaxed only if those of its communist adversaries increase. This has been fully appreciated in Peking, which finds itself in exactly the same position: in order to relax it needs, at the very minimum, to liquidate once and for all, the "Chiang Kai-shek clique" and whatever influence on Chinese affairs the government on Taiwan still has. One can guess that elimination of pro-Western governments in Southeast Asia and, perhaps, in Korea, the Philippines and Japan would also be desirable from Peking's point of view. Being practical men, the communist leaders of China are not trying to make all their desires subject to negotiation with the United States. Taiwan, however, they claim as their own and it would be very foolish to think that they do not mean it.

There is little wonder, therefore, that the relations between the two countries are what they are and that the United States is fixed on its policy of nonrecognition. Now the question is how this policy can be modified and what can be done to bring the positions of the two countries closer together. This question presumably has to be answered by the critics of the government policy. While considering their proposals, we should bear in mind they are limited to the United States' position: no one has yet offered any advice to the Peking government on how to modify *its* stand. This is important, for here we see not an effort to find some common ground for the two conflicting parties but an effort to make the United States' position acceptable to Peking, which has retained and in all probability will continue to retain its views on the subject.

What can the critics propose under such conditions? Their predicament is described by David Nelson Rowe:

> It would be a politically foolhardy person who would openly advocate the takeover of Taiwan by the Chinese Communists. Thus the movement toward accommodation with Communist China now takes the form of the "two Chinas" proposal, under which we are urged toward full relationships with Communist China while retaining Taiwan under our protective wing. That this policy has no possible chance of success does not seem to influence its advocates.[114]

The "two Chinas" solution means that the United States recognizes the communist government of China as that of the mainland while retaining relations with the Nationalist Government of China with jurisdiction limited to Taiwan and the Pescadores. Under such a solution the off-shore insular groups of Quemoy and Matsu would have to be handed over to the communists.

The "two Chinas" proposals have been by no means uniform. For instance, Arthur H. Dean recommended making recognition conditional on certain concessions on the part of the communists. He also felt that Communist China has to be admitted to the United Nations as a new member and that the Nationalists should retain the permanent seat of China on the Security Council.[115]

The authors of the Conlon Report, as we have already seen, suggest that, in return for recognition, the Peking regime should consent to the unification of Korea under the control of the United Nations.[116] Thomas K. Finletter thinks that a "two Chinas" solution should be part of a package deal which would consist of,

43

(1) a resolution on terms acceptable to us of all existing disputes between the non-communist world and communist China; (2) a commitment by the Peking regime to give up its policy of expanding its frontiers by force, direct or indirect; and (3) further commitments by the Chinese communist government to work with the United States and the Asian countries to reduce tensions everywhere. . . . An overall settlement with communist China should include not only a definite peace treaty ending the Korean War on terms acceptable to the United States and other United Nations countries, but also an arrangement for a unified and independent Korea whose safety would be guaranteed by the United Nations.[117]

Mr. Finletter believes that as a part of such a deal the United States should also get back all American prisoners from the communists, and that Communist China must accept a disarmament plan satisfactory to the West. As to the United Nations, the China seat in the Security Council should be given to India while both Chinas would be seated in the General Assembly as equals.[118]

The critics of nonrecognition tend to feel that legal grounds for turning Taiwan into a separate state are sufficient. For instance, such an authority on international law and relations as Quincy Wright, says that:

The United States is free to recognize Formosa and the Pescadores as an independent state under the Nationalist government. . . provided free and fair elections indicate that an independent state of Formosa under the Nationalist government conforms to the wishes of the inhabitants.[119]

The promoters of the "two Chinas" solution insist that Taiwan is not really a part of China. For instance, Finletter says that "the rights of the Formosans. . . . depend on the Japanese Peace Treaty by which Japan ceded Formosa and the Pescadores, but did not state who was to get them." Finletter thinks that the future of Taiwan has to be decided either by the 48 countries which signed the San Francisco Treaty or by the United Nations.[120] This contention, however, seems to rest on rather weak ground. Although the Nationalists did not sign the San Francisco Treaty, they made a separate peace with Japan dated April 28, 1952, according to which "all treaties, conventions and agreements concluded before December 9, 1941, between Japan and China have become null and void as a consequence of war." This includes the treaty of 1895 under which Formosa was ceded to Japan. This means, then, that since the cession was null and void as a result of the war, Formosa was returned to China, the same as all other Chinese territories, including Manchuria, once held by Japan. So it seems incontestable that Taiwan, under international law, belongs to China. As for which China, this is a question that makes sense only to the outsiders, since both the Communists and the Nationalists wholeheartedly agree that there is only one China. As John K. Fairbank puts it,

> Chinese politics for two thousand years has been focused on the unity of all Chinese under one rule. The Anglo-Saxon concept of "two Chinas" has been denounced by practically everyone from Chou En-lai to Chiang Kai-shek. . . .[121]

Even on the relatively minor subject of the disposition of the off-shore islands, we discover the same unanimity between the two warring camps of China. Chou En-lai said:

> As to Quemoy and Matsu, whether or not Chiang Kai-shek's troops withdraw from these islands is China's internal affair; it is an issue of civil war between the Central Government of New China and the Chiang Kai-shek clique. Even Chiang Kai-shek said that U.S. Senator Kennedy had no right to meddle in this question, to interfere in China's domestic affairs.[122]

One can be surprised to find out how large is the agreement between the Communists and the Nationalists. Allen S. Whiting says that:

> There is vigorous unanimity between Nationalists and Communists in asserting sovereignty over Tibet, in marking territorial boundaries around the South China Sea, and in asserting prerogatives of overseas Chinese. There is similar unanimity on the question of "two Chinas," both sides insisting that Taiwan and all its accompanying islands are inalienably Chinese and not subject to international negotiation or supervision.[123]

This unanimity between the implacable foes may look strange to the Western mind; it appears quite logical, however, to those who know more about China. Paul M. A. Linebarger points out that Peking and Taipeh (Chiang's capital on Taiwan),

45

both claim not to be two Chinas but to be one China. Each alleges that the other does not exist except at the most brutal level of raw, unjust, and unrefined fact. [Communists pretend] that the unfortunate island of Formosa is held by a mixture of American gangsters and renegade Chinese thugs and that with Chiang's death the island will return to the Communist motherland. The process of this strange form of political warfare through reduplication is thoroughly familiar to every Chinese who is at all articulate and is over twenty years old.[124]

The authors of the Conlon Report, who are aware of the existence of the "one and indivisible" China concept, point out that:

We must accept the fact that basic agreement between the United States and Communist China on such issues as Taiwan and Korea is inconceivable under any conditions at present.[125]

A British historian and political writer, Hugh Seaton-Watson, says:

I would like to see [the "two Chinas" solution carried out]. But it is inconceivable that Communist China would ever accept it.[126]

But how about Nationalist China? For the most part we have kept that actor of our drama in the background. This has been a common case. To many good people anxious to see the problem solved, the views of the Nationalist Chinese do not appear particularly relevant. They are tempted to assume that the dependence of the Chiang Kai-shek regime on American aid and protection gives the United States an upper hand in implementing whatever policy it sees fit to adopt. We have seen enough of the attitude of the Peking leaders towards the Nationalists. It might be worthwhile to note the attitude of the Nationalists toward the Communists, and the hopes still nurtured on Taiwan. Here is one view, as expressed by Chiang Kai-shek:

The Communists have not destroyed [the National Government of China], and they are beginning to realize that they may never win. It is difficult for them to accept a policy of patience toward us, just as it is difficult for many other people [on our side] to be patient about recovering the mainland. . . . We can never win if we fight merely as one Government against another. We can win only if the

46

Chinese people turn to us again. . . . We are ready to lead the Chinese revolution when it becomes active again. The Communists know this and they know that there is no power on heaven or earth which can stop us.[127]

It has been easy in the West to brush off this position as a nuisance, as an obstacle to a desirable settlement. Yet, brushing it off does not dispose of a very real factor in the situation. With a very efficient government, oversized armed forces, and its eleven million inhabitants enjoying one of the highest standards of living in Asia, Taiwan *is* a factor to be reckoned with. To ignore what is left of the Republic of China would be a foolish, indeed unforgivable, mistake. Rowe warns against taking Chiang Kai-shek for granted:

It is. . . certain that the Republic of China on Taiwan would break with us if we were to enter into relations with Communist China.[128]

The United States government feels the same way:

The Republic of China. . . could be expected to resist such arrangement with all means at its disposal. . . Peiping, too, would reject such an arrangement. . . There is no prospect that it would ever acquiesce in any arrangement which would lead to the permanent detachment of Taiwan from China.[129]

There have been suggestions to place Taiwan under some form of the United Nations trusteeship with international guarantees of the inviolability of its territory. Such suggestions usually gain in popularity in the United States whenever a recurrent crisis develops in the Taiwan area. This reflects an ever-present temptation to avoid a head-on clash with the adversary by simply dumping an apparently unsoluble problem on the world organization in a hope that "a dispute, by being put on the agenda of an agency of the United Nations would somehow lose its sting and become susceptible to a peaceful settlement which could not be otherwise obtained. . . as though there were in the United Nations a healing power which need only be invoked to make itself prevail."[130]

No less difficult is the problem of carrying out the "two Chinas" concept in the United Nations. The Republic of China's resistance to the removal of its representative from the Security Council by all its disposable means can be taken for granted. The view of the Peking regime on this subject is expressed by Chou En-lai:

> If the so-called "Taiwan Clique" is to appear in the United Nations, under whatever form and in whatever name — be it the Chiang Kai-shek clique or some other clique — we will definitely refuse to take part in the United Nations and sit together with them, so as not to create a situation of "two Chinas." This applies also to our participation in other international organizations and conferences.[131]

One could continue quoting such statements *ad infinitum*. However, this would be useless for they all point to the same stumbling block: that any solution smelling of "two Chinas" is completely unacceptable to both rival regimes and that there is no conceivable way to make them accept such a solution. This is confirmed by the critics of the American China policy themselves.[132-133]

Since the American government is not prepared to concede Taiwan to the Communists, where does this leave the critics? Some of them propose that the United States make a gesture of extending its recognition anyway — knowing full well that it won't be accepted — to enable the the United States to please its foreign critics. This would be a nice gesture, the people would say, and not really a big concession on the part of the United States. Such a suggestion, however, is rejected by those of the critics who are familiar with the situation in the Far East. A. Doak Barnett cautions:

> Under these conditions, if the United States were to extend full de jure recognition to the Peking regime only to have Peking refuse to reciprocate, there would be little or nothing gained, while losses might be substantial.[134]

Arthur H. Dean warns against attempts to move in the direction of meeting communist demands in general:

> If anything should be established from our past parleys with Communist countries, it is that gratuitous concessions induce further and more extravagant demands from them rather than mollifying their existing claims. This is fundamental.[135]

Thus we see how the critics of the American China policy are caught in contradictions. They are unhappy over the present state

48

of affairs. At the same time they fail to offer any workable alternative. Nonrecognition is bad. Recognition is impossible. Yet, they continue to insist that something must be done because the situation is getting increasingly dangerous. The authors of the Conlon Report say:

> Chinese nationalism is presently both adamant and arrogant, as is illustrated by Tibet and also by the border controversies with India and Burma.[136]

Barnett predicts more danger in the future:

> As its power grows, Peking may be tempted to exert increasing pressure on its weak neighbors, and if it believes it can use force to make local gains without fearing large-scale war, it may do so.[137]

And he adds:

> It is eminently clear that Communist China represents the most dangerous threat to American political and economic, as well as security, interest throughout Asia. . . . The Chinese Communists frankly state that their hope is ultimately to eliminate American influence entirely from the Western Pacific.[138]

The Conlon Report is no less gloomy. It advises that a policy of waiting for some break may be the best available for the moment but laden with danger. But it expresses grave doubts about continuing such a policy. And it warns:

> It is very questionable as to how long we can hold Communist China in check with a policy of containment through isolation.[139]

And so it goes, leaving the critics nowhere. What they propose in practical terms is almost anticlimactic:

— Let things take their natural course at the United Nations, do not attempt to block the seating there of the Chinese Communist representatives, and see what happens;

— Abolish embargo on trade with Communist China;

— Try to arrange an exchange of newsmen;

— Encourage cultural exchanges;

— Evacuate the off-shore islands;

— Accept "intellectually" the fact that the communists do

rule the China mainland and get used to putting up with their bad behavior.

This does not appear to be a cohesive alternative to the policy of nonrecognition. Yet, it represents a set of measures, the sum effect of which would be a softening of the American position *vis-a-vis* the Peking regime. If, as a result of these half-measures, Communist China becomes "intellectually acceptable" to the American people, the main obstacle to recognition would be eliminated. It can also be foreseen that this shift in public opinion would enable the champions of the "final solution" in the Far Eastern area to carry through a policy leading to the end of the efforts to contain Communist China in Asia — and to the abandonment of the "Chiang Kai-shek clique" to its own devices.

One difficulty to such a course is that the Chinese Communists themselves do not seem to appreciate the possibilities which it opens to them. Their steadfast refusal to cooperate in a program aimed at mollifying the American public opinion puzzles many people unfamiliar with the communist way of thinking, and who are reluctant to believe in the sincerity of communist assertions that they will eliminate the "capitalist way of life" from the face of the earth. Compromise, which is one of the essentials of a democratic society, is completely alien to a society based on communist ideology. The Chinese Communists are not interested in American concessions unless these concessions could be clearly presented to the world as an American surrender. They are not interested in fostering American tolerance of their bad behavior; they want us to recognize publicly that their behavior is good.

SINO-SOVIET RIFT

The argument that recognition of Communist China would help to create — or widen — a rift between that country and the Soviet Union, which, in turn would serve the purposes of the United States is a curious one. It comes almost exclusively from people who normally refuse to recognize the ideological nature of the communist threat to Western civilization and who prefer to view the East-West struggle as a manifestation of traditional power politics. They explain the aggressiveness of Communist China in terms of a pursuit of limited, even justifiable national goals and steadfastly refuse to get emotional over communist assertions that they will "bury" the capitalist world.[140] Guided by a sincere desire to build a more decent international society, these people are usually willing to go more than half way towards meeting "legitimate" demands of the communist regimes, hoping thus to achieve so much desirable *rapprochement* and a relaxation of world tensions. And it is exactly the same people who promote in the United States the idea of a possibility of the Sino-Soviet split. The point can be illustrated by the case of a prominent scholar who says that he shares "the general American aversion to Communism" but does not think that "this feeling should dominate national policy or individual judgment,"[141] and who, at the same time suggests that:

> Our tactics in power politics toward the Moscow-Peking axis should be divisive. . . . The Sino-Soviet partnership is not psychologically indissoluble.[142]

The authors of the Conlon Report, some of whom have long been on record as favoring accommodation with Communist China, say:

> The long-term solidarity between the U.S.S.R. and Communist China is by no means assured. . . . Increased strain upon Sino-Soviet relations due to some combination of factors is very possible.[143]

The editors of the Journal of International Affairs, who came out for speedy recognition of the Peking regime, suggest:

> Diplomatic recognition, normal trade relations, a seat in the United Nations, and perhaps some economic aid would give China an alternative to her close relationship with Russia and would provide an atmosphere in which latent frictions could develop into significant disputes.[144]

The argument is further developed by Professor Lincoln P. Bloomfield:

> It can be speculated that with the passage of time a common interest may develop between the Soviet Union and the

51

United States with respect to Communist China. It is possible that increasing strains between the two Communist giants will culminate in a collision of national and ideological interests comparable to that between Rome and Byzantium. The way in which Western planners evaluate this prospect should be a major determinant in estimating the value of having China in or out of the United Nations.[145]

Thomas K. Finletter, while not getting deeply into speculations as to the extent of the Sino-Soviet differences, warns that,

> there is a danger that by refusing to recognize (the Peking regime) we will be driving the Chinese communists and the Russians closer together.[146]

Another prominent critic of the nonrecognition policy, Chester Bowles says:

> Whatever may be said for America's present policy of refusing to agree that the Chinese government is an established fact, it certainly cannot be said to encourage the growth of whatever potential differences may exist between Peking and Moscow. . . . Sooner or later. . . the built-in strains between a dynamic, developing China and a suspicious, insecure Soviet Union are likely to be felt.[147]

Bowles speculates that the internal problems of Communist China may induce it to demand that the Soviet Union open Siberian lands to the excess Chinese population (although "Siberian lands" are no good for cultivation to begin with, and although the Soviets have a permanent food crisis of their own). Other writers point out significant ideological differences between Peking and Moscow, their competition in newly-emerging countries, the Chinese efforts to obtain a nuclear capacity of their own, and other areas where strains might conceivably develop between the two.

This group of critics — which forsees a "Titoist" role for the Chinese Communists and seeks to exploit the possibilities for wooing them away from Moscow — represents only one subdivision of the "Sino-Soviet Rift' school. Another subdivision, represented most prominently by Harrison E. Salisbury of *The New York Times* and Marvin L. Kalb of the Columbia Broadcasting System envisages a situation where the growing "yellow peril" of Communist China would create a basis for a Soviet-American *rapprochement*. Those who subscribe to the latter theory insist that, pressed by the belligerency of its Chinese allies, the Soviet leadership would eventually come to realize a substantial identity of the Soviet and American interests. They seek to bring this about by adopting a "softer" line in the United States policy toward the Soviets and by encouraging whatever liberal tendencies they manage to detect in Moscow.

One would think that there is an irreconcilable contradiction between the two viewpoints, that wooing Mao Tse-tung away from Khrushchev would require a policy quite different from that which would be aimed at wooing Khrushchev away from Mao. This, however, is lost on the critics. For instance, Marvin L. Kalb recommends that,

> we should adopt a highly flexible foreign policy aimed at exploiting the divisive pressures in the alliance so that Moscow and Peking will be deprived of the opportunity of facing the United States as a united team.[148]

In order to achieve such a commendable goal, "a highly flexible foreign policy," according to Kalb, should include recognition of the Peking regime. This would serve the United States purposes because it would show "the uncommitted world that we do not 'fear' Communist China" and because "it would rid us of our barren policy of nonrecognition, freeing our hands and minds for some imaginative diplomatic offensives." Kalb does not go to the trouble of using his own imagination as to what these "diplomatic offensives" should consist of. The best he can offer is that the American recognition of Communist China, coupled with the American-backed effort to seat Peking's representatives in the United Nations "would place the Communists on the defensive for the first time in many years." And he adds, that "Moscow and Peking would be puzzled by our change in attitude."[149]

That Moscow and Peking would indeed be puzzled by such an attempt by the United States to act against its own interests, cannot be questioned — while Kalb's line of reasoning definitely can. According to him, recognition of Communist China has to be accompanied by a massive education program in America with the purpose of preparing "the American people for the bitter, desperate struggle that we surely face with China — whether China remains allied to Russia or not."[150] Why, then, recognize the Peking regime, thus enhancing international prestige, letting down American allies in Asia and giving the Chinese Communists an opportunity to manipulate in the United Nations against the United States? These questions are left unanswered by the latter day Machiavellis. It is not surprising, therefore, that the promoters of the "Sino-Soviet Rift" theory are strongly challenged by students of communist world strategy who caution us not to be too optimistic over the prospects of the fight within the communist bloc. Philip E. Mosely states:

> Shared political and strategic objectives provide the strongest incentive for both partners. . . to bridge over even major conflicts of ideological outlook or economic interest. Those who believe that the Moscow and Peking centers can be separated from each other must, it would seem, prove either that their goals are incompatible or that each of the two centers may judge itself better able, in separation or even in conflict with the other, to achieve its own goals.[151]

Commenting on recent ideological frictions between the Soviet and Chinese Communists, William J. Jorden, who has spent many years in the Far East and in the Soviet Union reporting for *The New York Times*, says:

> The prospect of ultimate conflict or schism between the two big centers of Communist power can be of only limited encouragement to the rest of us. It seems highly unlikely that Moscow and Peiping would permit their dispute to get out of hand soon. The forces that unite them, their dogma, their shared hatreds, their suspicions, insecurities, and ambitions, — all tend to bring them together against what they consider their primary and most hostile foe. China, cut off from Soviet economic assistance and military support, would face incalculable troubles. For the Soviet Union, an open break with Peiping would be a tremendous setback, something she could only contemplate with alarm.[152]

The Department of State has taken a similar position on the "Chinese-Russian rift," as related to the issue of recognition:

> It would seem unrealistic to believe that recognition of Peiping by the United States or any other leading nation would have the effect of tempting the Chinese Communists to play a "Titoist" role.[153]

This view is supported by Professor Kissinger:

> Of course, the possibilties of a rift [between the Soviet Union and Communist China] must not be overlooked.

And if it occurs, we should take advantage of it rather than force the erstwhile partners into a new alliance through intransigence. Yet this is a far cry from the proposition that we can promote a split. In 1948 no Western policy could have set itself the goal of encouraging Tito to break away from Stalin. The attempt to do so might have been the best way to prevent it. Similarly, our diplomacy cannot have as a goal what we can only treat as a fortunate event.[154]

Kissinger's — and Mosely's — views are fully shared by none other than Chou En-lai, the Prime-minister of the communist government of China:

The Communist parties and the governments of China and the Soviet Union. . . believe in Marxism-Leninism and formulate their policy by integrating the principles of Marxism-Leninism with the specific conditions of their respective countries. Having the same belief and the same system, they share the same over-all principles and go along the same general direction. . . . This is not equivalent to saying that the two parties have no differences in the way they look at certain questions, nor does it mean that there is no difference in emphasis in the policies of the two countries. . . [but they] are as one in their opposition to imperialism and to. . . imperialistic policies. . . . Should the imperialists try to seek any loopholes for driving a wedge and sowing discord among the Socialist countries, they would do so in vain and are doomed to failure.[155]

Donald S. Zagoria of the RAND Corporation, who studied Sino-Soviet frictions in Asia, Africa and Latin America says:

Despite these points of friction, it must be emphatically stated at the outset that the Sino-Soviet relationship in underdeveloped areas, as elsewhere, continues to be marked by a powerful if not overriding community of ideology and mutual hostility to the West.[156]

Any new rumors about Soviet-Chinese frictions usually receive great attention in the West and make big headlines. There are, however, serious reasons to avoid basing any long-range policy on such rumors. One such reason is suggested by Suzanne Labin and Christopher Emmet:

To regard [the Sino-Soviet] frictions as symptoms of a profound rift is to indulge in dangerous wishful thinking.

Short of some final break, the greater the friction between Russia and China, the more will Moscow and Peking be likely to conceal it. Conversely, if the alliance is solid, both powers will stand to gain by giving the impression that they are divided. They can accomplish this best by precisely what they have been doing — issuing official statements of unity while "leaking" hints of disunity.[157]

One such "leak" was apparently made in February 1961 when Edward Crankshaw reported what was purported to be a documented summary of the disputes between Khrushchev and Mao Tse-tung. Commenting on Crankshaw's report, Paul Wohl of the *Christian Science Monitor*, writes:

> Serious doubt exists as to the accuracy and authenticity of the documents which recently inspired a worldwide interest in an allegedly serious rift between the Soviet Union and Communist China. Indeed, there is much internal evidence in the documents which indicates that they may be deliberately planted frauds. . . . The documents. . . are believed to represent a deliberate leak on the part of the Soviets.[158]

After analyzing the contents of the "documents" Wohl comes to the conclusion that "the purpose of such a leak would seem to be to convince the West that Moscow is under pressure from Peking and that Chairman Mao and his associates represent a danger to world peace. The West, under such circumstances, might be more inclined to pay a price for Premier Khrushchev's good services in restraining the Chinese fire-brands.[159]

Another round of speculations as to a possible split between Moscow and Peking was started early in July 1961 by another British expert on communist affairs, Isaak Deutscher, who presumably had come into possession of data indicating Khrushchev's fierce hostility toward Mao Tse-tung. Although authenticity of this data has been questioned by practically all informed sources, Deutscher's revelations gained wide coverage in the Western press. This prompted Professor Zbigniew Brzezinski of Columbia University to write in his letter to *The New York Times* on July 16:

> I am disturbed by the tendentious manner in which some recent events relevant to the Sino-Soviet relationship have been presented to the American public. I strongly fear

that the persisting inclination of some journalists to exaggerate Sino-Soviet differences will in the end prevent the public from acquiring a sophisticated understanding of both the complicated nature and the limits of the admittedly serious Sino-Soviet disagreements.

A few days before, appearing on July 10 in the National Press Club, Secretary of State Dean Rusk declared that although there was solid evidence of tensions between the Soviet Union and Communist China, this evidence did not provide a sound basis for Western policy-making. The same opinion had been on one occasion voiced by Professor W. W. Rostow:

> It seems unlikely, given the complex of interests which now hold the alliance together, that Sino-Soviet ties can be broken by seductive offers from the West taken alone. In fact, a partial accommodation to the West, brought about while maintaining the present Sino-Soviet tie, would tend to give Peking the best of both worlds and diminish the pressure for serious alterations in the links which now bind Peking to Moscow.... The well-meant efforts to alter Peking's attitude by urging a place for it in the UN and by seeking an expansion of trade in no important respect increase the chance of a break in the Sino-Soviet alliance; on the contrary, they may make it a more acceptable foundation for Peking's conduct of external affairs, by diminishing some of its costs.[160]

Secretary Dulles gave his characteristic view on the alleged conflict between the Soviet and Chinese Communists:

> Perhaps, if the ambitions of the Chinese Communists are inflated by successes, they might eventually clash with Soviet Russia. Perhaps, too, if the Axis powers had won the Second World War, they would have fallen out among themselves. But no one suggested that we should tolerate and even assist an Axis victory because in the end they would quarrel over the booty — of which we would be part.[161]

*　　*　　*

Let us assume, for the sake of the argument, that there is a latent conflict between the Soviet Union and Communist China. Then a legitimate question to ask would be: what can the United

States do in order to bring this conflict into the open and exploit it in its own interests? It seems logical that in order to achieve this end the United States has to make up its mind as to which of the two communist regimes it wants to have on its side. If the aim is to bring the Peking government over to "Titoism", the United States should be able to offer it an alternative to what it already has or what it feels it can obtain under the present circumstances. A simple diplomatic recognition, even coupled with a seat in the United Nations, quite obviously won't do: it does not add up to much from Peking's point of view. Would, then, the United States offer a large-scale resettlement program for the excess Chinese population? Would it help China's industrial development so that it could become independent from the Soviet Union economically and militarily? Would it supply the Chinese Comunists with nuclear weapons, hoping that they would use them against the Soviet Union? Would it offer them Southeast Asia, Taiwan and Korea on a silver platter, so to speak? Nobody has yet spelled out how, exactly, the United States should proceed in wooing Communist China and turning it against the Soviets. The critics of the American China policy have been completely silent on that point.

Another — the Salisbury-Kalb — school which promotes the idea of the Sino-Soviet rift feels that the party to win over is not Communist China but the Soviet Union. Somewhat daringly, it assumes that there are large areas "where our interests coincide with Russia's"[162] — like in developing of backward countries of Africa, Asia and the Middle East, or in the preservation of the international peace. It also assumes that the Kremlin leaders are apprehensive over the growing power of China and that they are potentially receptive to the idea of a Soviet-American alliance against the Peking regime. That these assumptions run contrary to everything we *know* about Soviet policies, hardly requires any proof. But let us, again, for the sake of the argument, grant it. Then, an elementary logic would dictate that the United States need not worry about changing its China policy. On the contrary, the more hostility there is toward the Chinese Communists in America, the better. If the possibility of a Soviet-American alliance is to be explored, recognition of Communist China would surely destroy such a possibility. The always suspicious Soviet leaders would be bound

58

to refrain from any *rapprochement* with the United States if they had reasons to think that Washington is attempting to play both ends against the middle. The "flexibility" of the United States foreign policy, no matter how puzzling, would have only one effect: it would impel the Soviet leaders to keep patching whatever differences they might have with Peking and to rely on a familiar, albeit sometimes difficult, ally rather than attempt to plunge into the arms of a basically hostile "capitalist" adversary.

This points out the crux of the matter, namely that both subdivisions of the "Sino-Soviet Rift" school do not take into account the ideological nature of the conflict between the communists and the West. A communist is much more likely to trust and to work with another communist than with a "capitalist" whom he has sworn to destroy and who, as he rightly suspects, would like to see nothing better than the disappearance of all that smells of communism from the face of the globe. The case of Tito's Yugoslavia is unique. It has been a case of a small country, where the leadership has the support of the nationalistic-minded and basically anti-communist population *because* of the stand it has taken against Moscow encroachments. But even Tito, despite relative moderation of his internal policies, does not trust the West — or his own people — and prefers to ally himself with the communist-oriented "neutralists" and has his representatives in the United Nations vote consistently with the rest of the communist bloc. What has kept Tito "neutral" has been not so much the aid and the friendliness of the West as it has been his keen awareness of the dangers he would have faced the moment he reentered the orthodox communist world.

It is quite obvious that Mao Tse-tung is in an entirely different position. In the spectrum of communist ideology he occupies a position of extreme "left," filled with an implacable hostility toward the West. He has no fear of Moscow domination and his relative influence within the world communist movement is incomparably greater than that of Tito. Whereas Tito's strength within his country lies in his accommodation with the West, Mao's major source of strength lies exactly in the opposite: in the intensity of anti-Western feeling among the ruling elite and in the aggressiveness of his foreign policy.

The "Sino-Soviet Rift" school, all speculations aside, promotes an over-all weakening of the American position *vis-a-vis* the communist bloc. While one subdivision recommends softening of the United States attitude towards the Soviets, another demands the same softening towards the Chinese Communists. If disciples of this school ever come to have it their way, the result of their efforts is likely to be a softening all the way around. To some this might appear as a devious and possibly sophisticated approach. But to others it must look like playing with fire — and with this nation's destiny.

PROSPECTS

Perhaps there have been times in the past when those in the United States government concerned with the formation of foreign policy needed little more than a clear understanding of American interests. In such a happy era it would be possible to secure the desires of the United States in respect to other nations: by bringing force to bear upon hostile governments of small countries, by persuasion of friendly governments in one way or another dependent on the United States. If this was ever the case before, it is not the case any more. Along with the great democracies of Europe, the United States has voluntarily subscribed to a code of international behavior which makes it exceedingly reluctant to use force, economic pressures or even the inducements of aid, in order to attain certain desirable goals. The smaller countries, thanks in part to the existence of the United Nations, where they can speak up without any restraints, have grown increasingly defiant of great powers. They are both seen and heard, and tend to make demands where, in the past, they had to beg. If it suits their interests, they threaten to — and actually do — ally themselves in part or in full with the international forces led by the Soviet Union, thus subjecting the West to blackmail and extracting concessions which otherwise would be impossible to obtain. The satisfaction of having one's will imposed on weaker neighbors can be claimed these days only by the Soviet Union and Communist China. Other major powers are compelled to negotiate and seek solutions acceptable to the parties involved whenever they desire to have something done. This has been true in relations between the countries belonging to the so-called free world. This has been doubly true in relations between the West and the communist bloc.

The *impasse* in negotiations with the communists which has characterized all Western efforts to solve particular problems in the post-war years is due to the fact that there are few solutions which are acceptable to both sides. The United States government has become aware of it, and if it nevertheless keeps trying, it is mainly because pressures for a negotiated settlement have been great and because so much of today's diplomacy has degenerated into propaganda.

This situation is rarely recognized by those critics of the United States who refuse to see the implications of the continued polarization in world politics. There are many intelligent people in America who claim to know better than the communist leaders themselves what is good for communists. These people brush off ideological differences as insignificant. They believe that such inducements as trade or economic aid are significant in relations with the communist bloc. They think that disarmament in the nuclear age must be uppermost in the minds of the communist leadership. They are convinced that relaxation of international tensions would be welcome in Moscow and Peking, for it would enable the communists to concentrate on peaceful development of their economies and building a happy socialist society.[163] Having ascribed all these and other motivations to Khrushchev and Mao Tse-tung, these people assume that mutuality of interests in the world is a fact and that, therefore, a political settlement is perfectly possible. If it has not been worked out so far, it is because the policy-makers in the United States government have been either stupid, stubborn, backward, or insufficiently flexible.[164]

Are the relations between the United States and Communist China in such a sad state only because of the failure of American decision-makers to recognize possibilities for an improvement? Or is it because of some silly communist intransigence which can and should be overcome by the power of Western reasoning? Or is it because of the peculiar communist Weltanschau which we fail to appreciate, that we are where we are? One can detect affirmative answers to these questions in many writings on international relations. Yet, at least some studies indicate that the roots of the Sino-American conflict are much deeper than it appears on the surface and that they include both ideological and power considerations. W. W. Rostow states:

> Chinese Communists have long regarded the United States as the key "imperialist" enemy of Communist expansion. . . . Communists sensed that, whereas in the long run Britain and France would be relatively weak in Asia, United States power would remain impressive over the foreseeable future.[165]

This prospect, Rostow suggests, has been appreciated in Peking for many years.[166]

In the words of Chou En-lai:

> It is the imperialist policy of the U.S. Government, and not merely the fact that U.S. troops have invaded and occupied China's Taiwan, that has put the U.S. Government in the position of being the enemy of (Asian) peoples.[167]

The accusation that the United States is pursuing an "imperialist" policy in Asia is standard in all communist pronouncements. Being a "swear word" in the communist vocabulary, the use of the term "imperialist" signifies only that a clash of interests has been taking place. As Whelan puts it:

> In the mind of Peking's communist leaders the United States is *the* enemy both for ideological reasons and those of international politics. Everywhere in Asia, Peking's objectives have been consistent: to displace American influence and thus eliminate the chief obstacle and threat to China's expansion and political control.[168]

Once this attitude is properly appreciated, the tremendous obstacles to any meaningful negotiations with the Peking regime become apparent. This is a fact which the critics of the U.S. policy toward Communist China have been inclined to underestimate. The idea of negotiations, as seen by the West, is a search for a solution to a problem with a hope of reaching a settlement to which both sides contribute by yielding some in their positions. That this is not the case in negotiations with the communists has been established by the United States a long time ago:

> Our experience with these negotiations has demonstrated that the only *modus vivendi* that could be worked out with the Chinese Communists would be one based on surrender on their terms. These terms, when defined in their simplest form, are that the U.S. get out of the west Pacific and leave the countries of East and Southeast Asia to cope with Peiping as best they can, separately and alone. Considering the vast disparity in power and resources between Communist China and the other countries of the region, such a retreat from responsibility on the part of the United States would be fatal. Yet this, in essence, is what Peiping offers us as a basis for negotiation.[169]

Whelan sums up the situation in the following terms:

> At this juncture Peking seems less disposed than ever toward conciliation, and its actions cannot fail to deepen distrust in the United States. . . . In general, prospects for a fusion of interests on the international level seem at this time to be very remote. [170]

Professor Steiner, who calls for a "tolerable solution" of the China problem, suggests that,

> For practical purposes, the CPR and the United States consider themselves in a state of undeclared war; and, under these conditions, "relaxation of tensions" is unlikely to be produced by piecemeal approaches to the large number of contentious items remaining on the unfinished agenda of United States-CPR business.[171]

An ample illustration of the communists' indisposition toward "piecemeal approaches" — and the idea of conciliation in general — has been presented by the recent Laotian crisis and at the 14-nation conference in Geneva where the West has tried to solve that crisis through negotiations. All that this attempt has thus far produced is the humiliation of a political surrender coming on top of a military defeat of pro-Western forces in Laos. At no point has the communist leadership been disposed to compromise and to yield even the smallest of its gains. What might be of particular significance is that the West has not even been allowed to save face and to retreat with some semblance of dignity. This leads to another

63

conclusion, namely that a mere physical expansion does not satisfy communist powers; that they invariably capitalize on their victory in political and propaganda terms so that even a minor success in a limited and not-too-significant area would appear to the whole world as a triumph of communism over capitalism.

It has been said many times in the past that

> The American people, with a profound and well-founded aversion to communism anywhere, appear to have developed a particularly intense resentment against the Chinese Communists.[172]

Many foreign critics, especially in Great Britain, India, and Indonesia, and in some other countries which have been trying to find their place in a world contested by two super-powers, have been questioning whether American aversion to communism has a sufficient foundation. These doubts, shared by the American critics, have noticeably affected the trends in the United States. Whelan says:

> In recent years [American policy] seems to have undergone some modification suggesting possible passive acceptance of the *status quo* in the Far East. There can be no doubt that the United States has responded to continuing Chinese military pressures rather than been itself the initiator of these pressures.[173]

Such a development, however, has not and could not contribute to an improvement in the relations between the two countries. If anything, it has made them worse, for the very passivity of the United States has served as an encouragement to further encroachments on the part of the Peking regime. Despite extraordinary difficulties on the home front, the latter has managed to carry out a very aggressive foreign policy with almost complete impunity. The changes in American mood toward acceptance of the *status quo* have been half-hearted and quite insufficient to create a similar trend among the leaders of Communist China. To achieve that end, some of the critics have urged further concessions to Peking. Since, however, an open advocacy of concessions has been a political liability in the United States, it had to be presented in some veiled form. Thus we hear of how "barren" and "negativistic" American

China policy has been; how great have been the opportunities that the United States has missed because of it; how much have we alienated our allies through our intransigence. For example, Chester Bowles says:

> A realistic understanding with the present Chinese government. . . appears impossible under present conditions. What we can and must do, however, is achieve a greater measure of agreement on the whole East Asia situation with our *allies*, and, if possible, with the neutral nations of Asia and Africa. At present most of them believe that our position in regard to China and Formosa has been impossibly negative, and this leaves us politically and militarily isolated in a crucial and explosive area.[174]

The fallacy of this and similar statements becomes apparent if we consider a basic difference between the interests of the United States and those of its allies, not mentioning the neutrals. The United States is the only country of the West which has truly global commitments. It is the only Western country with vital defense interests in East Asia, whose defense perimeter runs from Korea and Japan through Taiwan and the Philippines to Southeast Asia. And it is the only major country which has its hands free, for in no way does it depend on favors of the Peking regime for its well-being. Great Britain has interests in preserving Hong Kong and in protecting its investments and influence in a number of countries of the Far East. It believes that this can be done only if it stays on speaking terms with Peking. In addition, it has to pay homage to the views of the governments of India and Ceylon, members of the Commonwealth and earliest protagonists of recognition of Communist China. The British government has also to consider growing pacifism in England — which is not as influential yet as it was in the 30's but, in some ways, it is worse: then pacifism was created by a general distaste for war, while now its main cause is a fear of the potential enemy.

There is another factor which makes the British approach very different from the American. Having lost its empire and being reduced to a position of a second-rate power, Great Britain is much more anxious to seek a *modus vivendi* with the forces of Communism than the United States, and anxious to adjust to the realities of the growing influence of the communists in areas where the most vital interests of Great Britain are located. These efforts have not profited much. The British experience in dealing with Communist China has been humiliating and unrewarding (and British trade there has climbed to a mere 76 million dollars in 1958) but having accepted the fact of their growing weakness they have learned to swallow their national pride. As one report puts it,

> The British. . . realize that they lack the physical power and resources to directly contest the aims of the Communist bloc. . . . Therefore — and perhaps understandably — they conceive their primary task at this particular juncture of history to be one of survival. To achieve this, they have adopted a policy of accommodation with the Communist bloc. They hope that by such a policy they will be able to buy time, thereby allowing new factors to enter the world balance of power. In support of this thesis, they usually cite the inevitability of a conflict between the USSR and China. To them, therefore, the path of wisdom is to assist, in every way they can, the emergence of the People's Republic of China as a new power center, hoping that as it gathers strength it will gain a greater sense of independence, perhaps even turning against its former mentor, the Soviet Union.[175]

Another ally, France, although still an American partner in the SEATO pact, has been squeezed out of Asia altogether after the loss of Indochina in 1954. It has nothing but bitterness left from that experience and believes that if it could not keep its position in that part of the world, nobody else can. France has also been worried over increasing Chinese meddling into its African affairs and over Peking's support of the Algerian rebels. As a result, the French have been more hindrance than help to the United States in the Far East. As for the difference between the interests of the United States and those of India, Indonesia, or Burma, it is too obvious to require any elaboration. In the final analysis, as the Korean War has shown, the United States may count on only the very limited help of its partners wherever its interests do not fully coincide with their own. The main function of the leading nation of the West is to lead. It often has to follow a lonely path, without trying to reach a full consensus in the Western "camp", without attempting to push the burdens of responsibility for action either onto its allies or onto the United Nations, without striving to remain popular with everybody and at all times. If an American action is successful, the allies and even the neutrals will go along. If it fails, the United States will be blamed anyway.

The growing reluctance on the part of the American allies to support the United States in any undertaking which is likely to lead to an increase of tension in relations with the communist bloc reflects the decline of their confidence in the West's ability to win the global contest. Conversely, misgivings about the future produce pressures for accommodation and readiness to pay for it by one-sided concessions to the communists, of which the recognition of Communist China is but one.

*　　*　　*

With all the change in the American attitude toward Communist China in recent years, there is still a very long way to go before the point of recognition of the Peking regime is reached. This can be seen if we compare the present with 1933, when the United States, after 16 years of "ignoring" the Soviet Union, decided to recognize it.[176] Whelan says:

> Americans in 1933 accepted recognition of Soviet Russia as a matter of course. It was not a political issue in the Presidential election of 1932. At best it lay on the periphery of the election campaign. Recognition was, in short, a politically acceptable course. There were no serious domestic risks to be taken.[177]

By contrast, as of 1961, recognition of Communist China remains one of the most controversial issues in the United States. A substantial part of the electorate bitterly opposes it and there are few politicians who can advocate recognition without running into serious risks. There are numerous citizens' groups of great influence which firmly oppose recognition. Among them are all veterans' organizations, the A.F.L.-C.I.O., American Farm Bureau Federations, and the Chamber of Commerce of the United States. The Catholic Church is solidly behind the policy of nonrecognition, and so are most Protestant organizations. Public opinion polls

(Gallup, November 1958) indicate that only 20 per cent or slightly more (22 per cent in the Fifth Congressional District of Minnesota early in 1960) favor admission of Communist China to the United Nations, while over 60 per cent oppose it. This is a decline from the years of the Korean War but it is still a formidable opposition.

By 1933 the Soviet Union was already "intellectually acceptable" to the great majority of the Americans. There had already been extensive trade relations between the two countries; and the United States, then in the depths of the Great Depression, was anxious to expand further. The pressure on the government from important business groups in favor of recognition of Soviet Russia was very substantial. There is little or no such pressure today for recognition of Communist China.

Finally, there existed in 1933 important international considerations. As Whelan points out:

> The emergency of Hitlerian Germany was considered in Washington as in Moscow, to be more a potential threat than an imminent one. The threat from Japan was already immediate and real. No doubt both of these disturbing political realities influenced the President's decision and quickened his interest in devising a system for preserving peace.[178]

All in all, in Whelan's words "each nation had tangible political assets to gain from rapprochement: each came to have the will to bring it about."[179] This is obviously not the case with the United States and China today.

*   *   *

The elections of 1960 brought to Washington a number of prominent people who for years had been advocating a revision of the American policy toward China. Some did it in passing, as a part of criticism of the policies of the Eisenhower administration in general. Others went into much greater lengths in stressing the need for a major review of United States attitude toward the Peking regime. These people moved into key positions in the White House, the Department of State and other agencies dealing with foreign policy. Although the change in the prevailing political philosophy on the key issue of how to deal with the communist

68

strategy was not too drastic, it was, nevertheless, a significant one. If the newcomers could have it their way, the "rigidity" which characterized the Dulles era would give way to "flexibility"; a new and fresh look would be tried; once-rejected remedies would be attempted.

Certain changes in the policy toward China were forecast by the presidential contender Kennedy during the election campaign. In an interview published in the *New Republic* on June 27, 1960, he said:

> One of the first things I would do is to bring Communist China into the nuclear test ban negotiations in the hope that this would lead to other things. . . . We would have to continue to indicate that we're not going to permit them to dominate Southeast Asia, that while we're glad to discuss Formosa we're still going to meet our treaty commitments.[180]

Kennedy's views were also expressed in a memorandum published in 1960:

> In view of the Peking Government's failure to free American prisoners, its aggressive designs and actions against Tibet and South Asia, and its unwillingness to guarantee the integrity of Formosa, there is strong reason to withhold recognition. I feel there is merit in the view that China should not be allowed to 'shoot its way' into the United Nations and thence to recognition by the United States. I do not see it as a moral issue primarily, but I do think that we have every right to expect reciprocal benefits from such recognition.[181]

We also remember the views that Kennedy expressed during the famous "television debate" with Nixon on the disposition of the off-shore islands of Quemoy and Matsu when he suggested that the islands are indefensible and recommended their evacuation by the Nationalist forces. Yet, at no point has Kennedy suggested that the United States might consider abandoning Taiwan. On the contrary, he has been stressing his determination to "meet our treaty obligations" and expressing a belief that a modification of the American position should bring material benefits to the United States.

Nevertheless, a degree of identity of views of the President and those of his aides whom he himself brought into the government and who believe that the cleavage between the United States and Communist China could be overcome through reasonableness and compromise, was to be expected. These people, partly because of insufficient knowledge of communism and communist strategy, keep hoping for eventual normalization of relations with the Chinese Communists. They underestimate a probability that Peking may simply not want to enter diplomatic relations with the United States. Whelan states emphatically:

> There must be specific incentives on both sides as a precondition to recognition. . . . No cohesion of interests exists today between the United States and Peking. . . . It may be argued that for purposes of domestic solidarity and the compulsion to assert its authority in the Communist "camp" China would not want recognition. . . . Ideological incompatibility seems, indeed, to be far too great a barrier for the Chinese to overcome.[182]

Rowe gives an additional reason for Peking's lack of interest in improvement of relations with Washington:

> They would rather have us surrender on the Taiwan issue, under the blackmail of an atomic war threat, rather than to make any kind of bargain with us. The open defeat of the U.S. in the current struggle, on any important and easily comprehended issue, is far more important to them than almost any matter of substance, including Taiwan. It is because many of our policy advocates do not recognize this that they constantly urge what to them are perfectly logical lines of bilateral bargaining in dealing with Communists.[183]

There is a possibility that circumstances would force the United States to modify its position further, in order to make it acceptable to the communists. An attempt conceivably could be made to erase the present Republic of China from the map and give it some other name. As Chester Bowles suggested:

> We could propose in the United Nations that a plebiscite be held on Formosa to determine whether the people there prefer independence under their own government to absorption into the Chinese Communist political structure. . . . Eighty percent of the people are Formosans with a fierce sense of independence.[184]

At present such a step seems unthinkable, and it is impossible on practical grounds, but further deterioration of the Western position in the world can make anything possible. Yet, if such deterioration takes place, it would be inevitable that the demands of the communists would grow, not diminish.

There is one factor, however, which is likely to put a strong check on the U.S. government's moves toward accommodation with Peking: the mood in the country. In the popular view there is always a point when a policy of compromise turns into a policy of surrender. Even if the administration were to pretend that recognition of Communist China did not involve a defeat of the United States, it is doubtful that it would be sufficient to convince the public to go along with recognition. Whelan suggests that:

> An era of general conditioning through informal ties would seem to be another prerequisite for recognition. . . . This would permit an adjustment of views and attitudes informally and establish the mood for more direct and fuller commitments on the official level.[185]

The American China policy was discussed by President Kennedy with the British Prime-Minister Macmillan during their meeting in April, 1961. According to an unconfirmed *Associated Press* report from London (published in the *Washington Star* on April 12) Kennedy told Macmillan that he would need at least 12 months to prepare the American people even for the idea of having Communist China in the United Nations. If this report is correct, it indicates that Kennedy, like Truman before him, tends to underestimate the latent anti-communist sentiment in the country. Congress remains overwhelmingly opposed to a modification of the China policy. On May 3, 1961, a resolution expressing this opposition was introduced in both houses of Congress. Under the pressure from the administration and the Democratic congressional leadership, this resolution was for some time shelved in the foreign relations committees. This might prevent its adoption during the current session but would probably cause resentment among congressmen and complicate further the already tense relations between the Congress and the White House.

In addition to the domestic opinion, the government has to contend with the views of pro-American governments and people all over the world who regard nonrecognition of Communist China as primarily a moral issue. This sentiment is sometimes elusive, but important nevertheless. To many people who oppose communism and to whom the United States appears as a natural leader of the forces of freedom, the American policy, besides being "realistic" must also be "right". They regard every American concession to the communists as a sign of continuing weakening of the West. Their disappointment, in turn, contributes to a rise of the neutralist feelings and it may yet one day create an atmosphere when everybody would just start jumping on the communist bandwagon. If that happens, the United States would have an ultimate choice between fighting a desperate war and submitting to a surrender; there would not be any other alternative.

*   *   *

There is one more argument in favor of recognition of Communist China which we have not discussed. This is the argument that recognition is "inevitable", sooner or later. Many fatalistically inclined people feel that there is no point in postponing the fateful decision while there still might be a chance that an early recognition would do the United States some good. Walker attributes the popularity of this argument to the skill of communist propaganda which has been using the Marxian thesis of the "ironclad laws of history" with considerable success. Whether this is so, is difficult to prove. But it seems that fatalism in politics and in international relations should have been inherently alien to a democratic society. So far, the United States has refused to accept a notion that its actions are predetermined by some superior force. As John Foster Dulles once said:

> The United States need never succumb to the argument of "inevitability". We, with our friends, can fashion our own destiny. . . . Of all the arguments advanced for recognition of the Communist regime in China, the least cogent is the argument of "inevitability".[186]

Yet, if a pattern of continuous defeats in American confrontations with the communist bloc establishes itself, the psychology of "inevitability" might set in among the Americans. Even as it is, more and more people have come to fear that communism might be the wave of the future, repulsive as it appears to those who cherish the ideals of Western civilization. The spread of the "inevitability" concept might lead to a situation where the majority of the American public would decide that all resistance is useless and that the conflict with the communists has to be settled regardless of the costs. If that happens, surrender would become unavoidable.

Such a development, however, does not appear likely at the moment. It is to be expected that the advocates of the "fresh look" at Sino-American (and Soviet-American) relations who came to work in the government under President Kennedy shall soon discover the complexities of United States foreign policy, the intricate interdependence of treaties this country has concluded all over the world, and the need to live up to global responsibilities. So long as the promoters of the idea of accommodation remain in positions of power in the government, costly mistakes are apt to be made: people hate to admit that they had been wrong. But one day the period of experimentation will end, the losses will be counted, and a search for the effective ways to deal with communism will begin in earnest. Whether this takes place under the present administration, or under the next, the day will come when the United States will adopt a policy so hard and unyielding that it shall surpass anything the late John Foster Dulles ever hoped to create.

Part Two

CHINESE REPRESENTATION IN THE UNITED NATIONS

Few of the problems which have vexed the United Nations over the years have been thornier than that of representation of China. The Second World War and the immediate postwar years left unsettled a number of situations in which two opposing governments are found within the same nation. In such cases division was not according to some ethnographic or economic principle, or because of the will of the people, but because the nation concerned lay athwart the line delimiting the extent of Soviet power at the end of the war.

The case of "two Chinas" is different from that of two Germanys. While it may be true that the Soviet Union played a major — if not decisive role in the victory of the Chinese Communists over the Nationalist forces, Communist China has not only succeeding in maintaining a substantial degree of independence but has gradually evolved into what appears to many a major world power. It has not succeeded, however, in subjugating the whole of China: the island of Taiwan and the insular groups of the Pescadores, Quemoy and Matsu have remained under effective control of the old Nationalist government. So long as the government of the Republic of China exists on Chinese soil and claims to represent the whole Chinese nation — a claim recognized by a majority of world governments — the state of civil war continues in China. At present, in addition to incessant propaganda warfare, the Chinese Civil War manifests itself in sporadic shelling of the off-shore islands by the Communists, in an effective blockade of the communist-held ports of Amoy and Foochow, in occasional Nationalist commando raids of the mainland and in Taiwan's support of anti-communist resistance along the Burmese border.

Despite the two governments' mutually exclusive claims to sovereignty over China the rest of the world is inclined to consider the war in China as finished. A great disparity in the size of the territory (3,760,000 sq.mi. vs. 14,000 sq.mi.) and the population (650,000,000 vs. 11,000,000) controlled by the warring sides, and other factors limiting the chances of Nationalist reconquest of the mainland of China, tempt outsiders to disregard the bitterness of the continuing conflict. The fact that the Republic of China's domain is separated from the mainland by sea and that the Kuomintang government survives primarily thanks to United States protection undermines the Nationalist claim to sovereignty over the whole of China even more.

Nevertheless, so long as Mao Tse-tung and Chiang Kai-shek agree on at least one point — that there is only one China and that that China includes Taiwan and the mainland, indivisible — the outside world is forced to reckon with a thorny problem, especially since the thesis of a "one and indivisible China" is supported by the whole might of the Soviet bloc. As far as diplomatic recognition is concerned, the governments of other countries are compelled to make their choice; as of the summer of 1961, fifty-four of them chose to continue recognition of the Nationalist government on Taiwan as the legitimate government of China, while thirty-seven established diplomatic relations with Peking.

This picture is reflected in the United Nations. The Republic of China was among the founders of the international organization, and was reckoned among the "Big Five" who received permanent seats in the Security Council. It was this government which first fell victim to Japanese aggression and which contributed heavily to the cause of the United Nations in the Second World War. True, the government's internal weaknesses prior to 1949 were generally condemned and the nature of its resistance to the Chinese Communists was met in many circles with something less than admiration. Nonetheless, China's neighbors had few reasons to complain about the behavior of the Chiang Kai-shek government, and its record both as a member of the League and of the United Nations has been unmarred by violations of the obligations of membership.

Communist China is in a peculiar position. It is headed by a revolutionary government which, in the eyes of those who oppose it, lacks legitimacy. The behavior of the Communist regime has in many fields been incompatible with the principles on which the

76

United Nations was founded and its leaders have made no effort to conceal their contempt for these principles. At the same time the regime has established its control over most of China to a degree undreamt of by any recent Chinese government. For the first time in modern history, to many the image of China is that of a major power. With the arrogance characteristic of a revolutionary regime, the communists demand international recognition and membership in the United Nations as their right. This demand presents those who hate and fear them with a challenge of the first dimension.

In the case of a revolutionary regime controlling a smaller country, such a demand would not have mattered much, for few governments would have cared, one way or another, and an international settlement would have been easier. But in a situation where Communist China is rapidly becoming an important element in the shifting balance of power between the communist camp and the West, every move which promises to enhance the fortunes of the one bloc at the expense of the other acquires a major importance.

By any objective test the appearance of representatives of Communist China in the United Nations would mean a major defeat for the United States and its allies, and a major victory for the Soviet Union and the Communist cause. More likely than not, it would start a chain reaction in the Far East and greatly strain the bilateral and regional alliances aimed at containing the might of Communist China. The spirit of the Charter of the United Nations would again be modified and the organization, abandoning the last vestiges of selectivity of membership, based on certain tests, would take a great step towards universality. With Communist China as a member, there would be no reason — or way —to deny admission to East Germany, North Korea, Outer Mongolia and North Vietnam. And the Republic of China would likely be the first member to be expelled from the organization — for is this not a condition set forth by the Mao Tse-tung government for its participation in the United Nations?

THE HISTORY

In cablegrams dated November 18, 1949, the Foreign Minister of the Central People's Government of the People's Republic of China informed the President of the General Assembly and the Secretary-General of the United Nations that his government repudiated the legal status of the Chinese delegation under Dr. T. F. Tsiang and held that it could not represent China. In another message of January 9, 1950, the Peking government demanded that Tsiang be expelled from the Security Council forthwith. The next day, the Soviet representative in the Security Council submitted a draft resolution which proposed that the Council should not recognize the credentials of Tsiang and to exclude him from the Security Council. The Soviet draft resolution was discussed at the meetings of the Council on January 12 and 13. During the discussion the representatives of Ecuador and Cuba took the position that since their governments continued to recognize the Nationalist government of China, they would insist that T. F. Tsiang, its representative, continue to represent China in the Security Council. The British representative suggested that until a majority of the members of the Security Council had recognized the new government in China it would be premature to discuss the Soviet draft resolution. The United States representative voiced the opinion that Tsiang should continue to represent China pending the Council's decision on the matter. He also stated that, in his view, the Soviet resolution "presents a procedural question involving the credentials of a representative of a member;"[1] as such it was not subject to veto.

Tsiang, however, argued that this was not a question of credentials, "but a question of representation. It is, therefore, not a question of mere procedure; it is a political question of the utmost importance." As such it would be subject to veto.

As it turned out, the question of whether the veto would be applicable did not have to be settled. There was no test. The Soviet resolution was rejected by the Security Council by a vote of 3 in favor (USSR, India, Yugoslavia), 6 against (China, Cuba, Egypt, France, Ecuador and the United States), and 2 abstaining (Norway and the United Kingdom). The Soviet representative then announced that he would not participate in the proceedings "as long as the representative of the Kuomintang group has not been excluded from the Security Council" and that his government would not recognize the legality of Council decisions taken in the meantime. He then left the meeting.[2]

In the following months, Soviet representatives walked out of almost 40 United Nations organs and specialized agencies, starting a boycott which was to last until after the outbreak of the Korean War. This boycott created a major crisis in the United Nations, a crisis which Secretary-General Trygve Lie attempted to solve. Believing that the deadlock in the Security Council on the issue of Chinese representation resulted from the fact that a majority of its members did not recognize the communist government of China, Lie circulated among the members a memorandum entitled *Legal Aspects of Problems of Representation in the United Nations,* in which he understook to define the relationship between "recognition", on the one hand, and "representation", on the other. Arguing from precedents of United Nations practice, he concluded that:

1. A Member could properly vote to accept a representative of a government which it did not recognize, or with which it had no diplomatic relations, and
2. that such a vote did not imply recognition or a readiness to assume diplomatic relations.

Further, if the new revolutionary government exercised effective authority within the territory of the state,

it would seem to be appropriate for the United Nations organs, through their collective actions to accord it the right to represent the State in the Organization, even though individual members of the Organization refuse, and may continue to refuse, to accord it recognition as the lawful government for reasons which are valid under their national policies.[3]

The Lie memorandum immediately drew a formal protest from T. F. Tsiang, who accused the Secretary-General of overstepping the bounds of his authority since the question of Chinese representation could not be held to threaten the maintenance of international peace and security within the meaning of Article 99 of the Charter, the only article that assigned a sphere of political action to the Secretary-General. Tsiang insisted that the "linkage between recognition and representation is only natural and inevitable," and concluded, that:

> The Chinese Delegation regards the Secretary-General's memorandum as a deliberate attempt to prejudice China's case before the United Nations. It oversteps the duties of the Secretary-General and undermines public confidence in his impartiality. . . . The memorandum is both bad law and bad politics.[4]

Not conceding defeat, Trygve Lie went to Washington where, on April 20, 1950, he met with President Truman and Secretary of State Acheson. He pleaded with Truman to abandon American opposition to the seating of Communist China in the United Nations. He suggested that Taiwan (Formosa) was under virtual occupation by the Nationalist forces and that the Formosans could conceivably want independence from China. If such were the case, Taiwan could be regarded as a separate state and there wouldn't be any issue in the United Nations. Truman remarked that "nobody could trust the communists" and refused to cooperate.[5] Dismayed at the lack of American acceptance for his plan, Lie went to London for help only to hear from Sir Gladwyn Jebb that, without active American support, His Majesty's Government could see no way of obtaining a necessary majority in the Security Council. Lie's visit to Moscow was even less productive.

In the absence of Soviet representatives there was nobody, for the time being, to champion the cause of Communist China in the United Nations. And by the time the Soviets returned, the launching of communist aggression in Korea — soon to be followed by direct intervention of Communist China in the Korean War — put Peking's claim to representation in the United Nations in a somewhat harsher light.

Truman's Executive Order of June 27, initiating steps designed to neutralize Taiwan, was met in Peking by violent expressions of determination to "liberate" the island and repel this American

80

"aggression". The communist government simultaneously demanded Security Council action against "aggressors". The Council discussed the Peking complaint late in November of 1950, in the presence of the Chinese Communist representative, General Wu. Wu demanded condemnation of "criminal acts" by the United States and the application of sanctions. A resolution to this effect, submitted by the Soviet Union, was defeated in the Council on November 30 by a majority of 9 to 1, the Indian representative abstaining for lack of instructions.

The Soviet representative, Malik, returned to the Security Council on August 1, 1950 to assume the chairmanship. He started his opening speech with a ruling that the "representative of the Kuomintang group seated in the Security Council does not represent China and cannot therefore take part in the meetings of the Security Council." This was immediately challenged by the American and British representatives. Sir Gladwyn Jebb quoted Rule 17 of the Rules of Procedure which states that "Any representative on the Security Council, to whose credentials objection has been made within the Security Council shall continue to sit with the same rights as other representatives until the Security Council decided the matter." Malik made a long speech but was unable to convince the Council. He was overruled by a vote of 8:3 (USSR, India, Yugoslavia, in the minority) and Rule 17 was sustained.[6] The issue, once the Security Council had disposed of it, could be introduced in the General Assembly. At the opening of the Fifth Session, the USSR and India proposed the seating of the Chinese Communist representative, and a General Assembly recommendation that other United Nations organs do the same. These proposals were overwhelmingly defeated. The General Assembly then adopted a Canadian resolution which provided for a Special Committee to consider the question of Chinese representation. The resolution stated,

> that pending a decision of the General Assembly on the report of this Special Committee, the reprerentatives of the National Government of China shall be seated in the General Assembly with the same rights as other representatives.[7]

The Special Committee was to present its conclusions after the general question of representation had been studied by the *Ad Hoc* Political Committee. This committee, although boycotted by the Soviet bloc did engage in lengthy discussions; however, it was unable to come up with anything better than a draft resolution which carefully hedged on the issue. This resolution was adopted by the Assembly on December 14, 1950, by a vote of 36 to 6, with 9 abstentions. In its essential part, it,

> . . . *Recommends* that whenever more than one authority claims to be the government entitled to represent a Member State in the United Nations and this question becomes the subject of controversy in the United Nations, the question should be considered in the light of the Purposes and Principles of the Charter and the circumstances of each case;
> . . . *Recommends* that the attitude adopted by the General Assembly. . . concerning any such question should be taken into account in other organs of the United Nations and in the specialized agencies.
> . . . *Declares* that the attitude adopted by the General Assembly. . . concerning any such question shall not of itself affect the direct relations of individual Member States with the State concerned.[8]

The resolution of December 14 was the only one ever adopted by the General Assembly which attempted to deal with the question of representation. As noted by Herbert W. Briggs, it "englobes everything previously argued and leaves the United Nations without precise guidance." Moreover, because of its wording it leaves open a possibility "that the Chinese Communists might be seated in some United Nations organs and the Chinese Nationalists in others."[9]

After the adoption of this resolution, the Special Committee on Chinese representation met, as provided for in the Canadian resolution. But by this time the Chinese Communists had intervened openly in Korea, thus creating an entirely new situation. Despite the efforts of Sir Benegal N. Rau of India, the committee chairman, to work out some solution, the committee eventually reported that it was unable to make any recommendations.

As the Korean War dragged on, the Western position on the question of Chinese representation became consolidated. The war also led to an emergence of an Asia-Arab group of 12-13 countries in the role of would-be peace-maker between the communist bloc and the West. Within the United Nations, the Security Council was rendered inoperative by the presence of the Soviet representative. To meet the needs of the situation, the General Assembly adopted, on November 3, 1950, the Uniting for Peace resolution. This resolution, among other things, allowed the Assembly to discuss questions which more properly should have been within the jurisdiction of the Security Council. Thus the Assembly was able, on February 1, 1951, to pass a resolution branding the Chinese Communists as aggressors,[10] and, three months later, a resolution recommending a strategic embargo on the shipment of war materials to Communist China and North Korea.[11] The latter resolution was subsequently implemented by 45 countries.

During 1950, United States policy toward the Peking regime steadily hardened. In May, Assistant Secretary of State Dean Rusk said:

> We recognize the National Government of the Republic of China, even though the territory under its control is severely restricted. We believe it more authentically represents the views of the great body of the Chinese people. . . . We do not recognize the authorities in Peking for what they pretend to be.[12]

Shortly after this, Secretary of State Dean Acheson, for the first time, indicated that the United States might resort to the veto in order to keep Chinese Communist representatives out of the Security Council.[13] In subsequent years, the United States repeatedly confirmed its intention to use its veto power for this purpose. Yet, in fact, it has never needed to do so, since the Soviets have made no further effort to unseat T. F. Tsiang in the Security Council.

This position, however, might be modified by the Kennedy administration. Appearing on the "Meet the Press" program on July 23, 1961, undersecretary of State Chester Bowles suggested that before using its right of veto in the Security Council, the United States would seek legal opinion of the World Court on applicability of veto in this case. If so, it would be an unprecedented development, for there is no provision in the Charter of the United Nations making a use of veto subject to a ruling of the World Court. So far, no great power has ever considered submitting its right of veto to such an arbitration. In this case, it appears as just another attempt on the part of the advocates of the "fresh look" to force through the seating of Communist China by dodging the issue and throwing the responsibility for protection of American national interests into the lap of an international organization.

In 1951, at the opening of the Sixth General Assembly Session, the USSR demanded that the question of Chinese representation be included in the agenda. The representative of Thailand then moved that the General Assembly postpone consideration of all proposals on Chinese representation for the duration of the session. The Thai resolution was carried by a vote of 37 to 11 with 4 abstentions.[14]

The expedient of postponing any discussion of the issue "for the duration of the session" has been used by the West with unfailing success ever since. Fears that the Chinese Communists might be seated in some organs of the United Nations and specialized agencies, while the Nationalists remained in others, did not materialize; all United Nations bodies have followed the recommendation of the General Assembly as expressed in the December 14, 1950, resolution and have adopted a uniform wait-and-see attitude. Whenever the USSR or India have attempted to unseat a Nationalist representative, such attempts have been easily defeated by a substantial majority of nations. Thus, as of the summer of 1961, Communist China remains excluded from all activities of the United Nations.

CRITERIA FOR REPRESENTATION

As we have seen, the United Nations faced the problem of Chinese representation the moment the Central People's Government of the People's Republic of China was proclaimed in Peking. Despite serious tensions which the communist seizure of power in China produced in the Far East and in the relations between the major powers, there was a persistent feeling in the United Nations Secretariat that the sooner the change of government in China was recognized the better the prospects for the United Nations, as a whole, to fulfill effectively its various functions. In some ways, this feeling resembled the League of Nations' attitude toward Germany in the early 1920s. As one historian says:

> Long before the international situation had become ripe for the entry of Germany into the League practically the whole Secretariat favored the step; not out of any pro-German sympathies but out of the belief that the absence of any major power was in itself an element of weakness, and that the spirit of war should be liquidated as soon as possible in order to begin the reconstruction of the world.[15]

It was, however, inevitable that the hopes for a speedy replacement of the Nationalists as representatives of China in the United Nations were frustrated. For, while the case of Germany was simply one of admitting another new member the legitimacy of whose government was questioned by no one, the present case was confused by the fact that there were two contenders for the seat of China, one of whom had already been in possession of this seat. Which government was entitled to represent China? What criteria of judgment should be applied to the case? The answers may have looked clearer at the beginning, but as time went by and the nature of the new government of China became clear in the course of the Korean War, the question of criteria grew increasingly more complex. Brigg says:

> The deceptively simple questions of the criteria to be employed in determining which of two governments is entitled to represent a Member of the United Nations in that organization and where the legal right to make that determination resides, appear, upon analysis, to be matters of great intrinsic complexity. These difficulties are intensified in the Chinese question by the profound distaste exhibited by a majority of the Members of the United Nations for communist regimes and Soviet tactics. . . and by the finding of the United Nations General Assembly that [Communist China] "by giving direct aid and assistance to those who were already committing aggression in Korea and by engaging in hostilities against United Nations forces there, has itself engaged in aggression in Korea."[16]

During the first years of the controversy, there was a noticeable temptation on the part of many people the world over to disregard the fact that there were still *two* rival governments of China. The resounding defeat of the Nationalists led to an expectation that the Chiang Kai-shek government on Taiwan would be short-lived and, abandoned by other nations, doomed to annihilation. In a book published in 1951, Hans Kelsen already considered as perfectly plausible an assumption that:

> The only government of the Republic of China under general international law is the communist government which is in effective control of the territory of China and its people.[17]

A year later, reflecting the view quite common in the United Nations circles, Herbert W. Bridges asserted flatly that:

> The long-range interests of the United Nations [cannot] be served by disregarding the unpalatable fact that the only government in effective control of China is the Chinese Communist government.[18]

The "long-range interests of the United Nations," as seen from the New York headquarters, appeared, however, to be in conflict with those of a majority of individual states. This was demonstrated not only in the heated atmosphere created by the Korean War but also in the years following the armistice. As Fred Greene points out:

> Exclusive reliance on objective criteria does not take into account the vehement reaction expressed in past decades against governments accused of aggression.[19]

To many member states the argument that the communist government was in "effective control" over the mainland of China seemed to be of minor significance. Even at an early stage, says Briggs:

> A clearly ascertainable majority opposed "effectiveness" as the sole criterion — even before evidence began to reach the General Assembly late in October, 1950, that the Chinese communist government had embarked upon a policy of overt aggression in Korea.[20]

And, as late as 1957, Assistant Secretary of State Walter S. Robertson took the view that the Peking regime did not represent the Chinese people.[21]

The Chinese aggression in Korea provided the opponents of Communist China with an argument of extraordinary dimensions. This intervention was a clear-cut violation of both the spirit and the letter of the Charter. The formal legal and procedural argument rapidly lost its force: in view of the majority of the United Nations' members it was a major *political* test that the Chinese Communists were failing to pass.

But the fact that in 1950 the Peking regime was waging war against the United Nations forces in Korea, or had been branded as an aggressor by the General Assembly did not alter the views of the Secretary-General.[22]

This view has persisted over the years. In 1960 A. Doak Barnett stated:

There is little merit in the idea that a nation, once branded an aggressor, should be permanently excluded from the community of nations.

Among the members of the United Nations such a position has been adopted by a number of the "neutralist" nations, notably India, Indonesia and Burma. Before the Chinese Communists intervened directly in the Korean War this position was also supported by Great Britain, which had recognized the Peking regime early in 1950. The British action was precipitated by anxiety over the fate of Hong Kong, by the hopes of salvaging substantial British assets in China and by pressure on the part of Indian Prime-minister Nehru.[24]

Still, it has been the Soviet Union which has remained in the forefront of the fight for the seating of Communist China in the United Nations. Soviet arguments in favor of such action have generally paralleled the reasoning of the Secretary-General and the "neutralist" governments. Yet, Soviet motivations, unlike those of Trygve Lie, have little to do with a desire to preserve and strengthen the United Nations. By presenting their demands for the entry of Communist China in a noisy and intemperate way, the Soviets tended to defeat their own purpose and to make the parallel efforts of the Secretary-General and his supporters more difficult of realization. In passing it may be stated that the Soviet tactics gave rise to speculations in some Western circles that the Soviets did not really want to see the Chinese Communists in the United Nations; this theory fitted with related speculations as to an imminent Sino-Soviet rift.

A sizeable majority of nations has successfully resisted all attempts to seat the Chinese Communists in the United Nations and to interpret membership clauses of the Charter too liberally. This majority has been led, from the start, by the United States. Its position was expressed by Secretary of State Dulles, who said that the Security Council,

> is the body which by the charter is entrusted with primary responsibility for the maintenance of peace and security in conformity with the principles of justice and international law. It would be grotesque if that high responsibility were to be conferred upon a regime which itself stands condemned as an armed aggressor against the United Nations and which itself is a most conspicuous violator of justice and international law.[25]

The Department of State, in a major statement, warned against ignoring the Communist record:

> For Communist China to be seated in the United Nations while still unpurged of its aggression and defying the will of the United Nations in Korea, would amount to a confession of failure on the part of the United Nations and would greatly reduce the prospects for future successful action by the United Nations against aggression.[26]

To those who argued that the presence of Communist China in the United Nations might have a beneficial effect on that government's behavior John Foster Dulles answered that "the United Nations is not a reformatory for bad governments."[27]

In the 1950's this stress on the moral aspects of the United Nations and the protestations of support for the spirit of the Charter carried considerable weight with many nations. Persistent violations of international law and order by the Peking regime, were roundly denounced from the rostrums of the United Nations. For the time being, a majority of member states chose to disregard a suggestion that "effective control" might be a major test for representation of a government in the United Nations. Reluctantly, Briggs conceded that, where two rival governments of a Member state request representation in the United Nations, United Nations organs should be entitled to choose between them on the basis, in part, of their adherence to the principles of the United Nations.[28]

REPRESENTATION vs. RECOGNITION

Little success was had with the argument initially advanced by Secretary-General Trygve Lie in his memorandum of March 1950, contending that the issues of representation in the United Nations and of recognition of Communist China by individual member states were, by nature, separated. Notwithstanding the need for a larger degree of international cooperation, the member states insisted on pursuing in the United Nations their national policies. To divorce from domestic considerations positions taken with respect to an important international issue proved to be impossible, particularly for democratic countries. There were fears in many places that the seating of Communist China in the United Nations would be the "back door" to general recognition of the Peking regime. The opinion that "UN representation has nothing whatever to do with diplomatic recognition"[29] has failed to gain acceptance. At least some legal authorities argue for an opposite view:

> If a community is admitted to the United Nations, all other Members — also those which have not yet recognized this community as a state and even those of them which voted against its admission — are under definite obligations in relation to this community as a state. . . . They would certainly violate the Charter if they would refuse to fulfill their obligations in relation to this community on the ground that it is no state and hence not a subject to international law. Consequently, admission of the community not yet recognized by some Members necessarily implies that these Members must consider the community as a state, which is essential function of the legal act of recognition.[30]

The author makes a distinction between recognition of a state — which in his opinion is automatic the moment it joins the United Nations — and establishment of diplomatic relations with it by other member states. The latter is decided by each member of the international community, individually. This latter act he considers to be of secondary importance, because establishment of normal diplomatic relations with the already recognized state "is recognition not in the legal, but in merely a political sense."[31]

The United States has apparently adopted this interpretation — that membership in the United Nations constitutes some form of recognition — and, as a result, has always stressed the connection between its own policy of non-recognition of Communist China and its position on the issue of Chinese representation in the United Nations.[32] Consistent with this position it has avoided any step which could be interpreted as recognition. Every time the United States has engaged in talks with the Chinese Communists, it has gone to considerable lengths to explain to the public that such talks do not imply any degree of recognition.

There are jurists, however, who disagree with the notion that the admission of a country to the United Nations makes its recognition by other members automatic. On the other hand, at least some of them appreciate the delicacy of the situation. Pitman P. Potter, editor of the American Journal of International Law states, for instance, that there is "little or no correlation between recognition. . . and membership in an international union." Yet taking into account the realities of the American political scene and possible international political repercussions, he concludes that,

> the opposition to substitution of Communist China for Nationalist China on the Security Council would be unsurmountable. We may be confronted here with a deadlock destined to endure for a decade or more. It would not appear that the United States should or could take a position other than the frankly temporizing one which — without great happiness or dignity, be it freely admitted — she is taking now. Politics, or the art of politics, especially international politics, consists of choosing between or among various different evils.[33]

CREDENTIALS

Suggestions have been made that the problem of representation of China in the United Nations could be reduced to that of credentials and be disposed of as a procedural matter. Inis Claude asserts:

> The seemingly interminable controversy over the representation of China in the United Nations bears out the conclusion that the treatment of membership question as a political and moral problem leads ultimately to the *confusion* of the issue. . . The Chinese question. . . is technically a matter of credentials.[34]

It is doubtful whether such a glossing over of the controversy can be sustained. The General (Credentials) Committee has only the power to examine credentials and report to the General Assembly; it has no power to decide the legitimacy of the government which issued the credentials. Neither the Charter of the United Nations, nor the Rules of Procedure, provides for a situation in which two governments — each of which is recognized by a number of member states — claim the right to represent one and the same member state.[35] The situation is complicated enough in the General Assembly, let alone in committee. As Kelsen points out:

> The Rules of Procedure of the General Assembly do not contain provisions by which, in case of two authorities claiming to be the government of a Member state, it could be prevented that the Heads or Foreign Ministers of both governments or the representatives accredited by each of the two governments — in contradiction to the provisions of the Charter — participate, at least provisionally, in the meetings of the General Assembly.

Kelsen suggests that a broader interpretation of the Charter is conceivable:

> If in case of a revolutionary change of government within a Member state the General Assembly or a Council ap-

91

proves the credentials of the representatives issued by the new government, all members of the approving body are bound by this decision, since the Charter may be interpreted to confer upon the General Assembly and the Councils the power to approve the credentials of the representatives of their members, which necessarily implies the power to recognize the government issuing credentials in case it becomes doubtful who is the legitimate government of a Member competent to issue the credentials of its representatives.[37]

It is obvious, however, that such broad treatment of the technical process of approving credentials endows this process automatically with a political susbstance; this, indeed, is exactly what has happened. Green says that,

by making Chinese representation a substantive issue, the United States has subjected it to the rule of great power unanimity in the Security Council and a two-thirds vote, rather than a simple majority, in the General Assembly. American reasoning can hold that the spirit of the Charter — symbolized by the veto — permits a great power to counter any action it considers damaging to its vital interests. . . . [This] official American stand is operating within the broad directives of the 1945 Charter.[38]

Treatment of the issue of representation as substantive by nature has been generally accepted in the United Nations. At the same time, few today would question the Kelsen assumption that criteria for membership must be decided by a collective act of the United Nations. Briggs says:

Where the credentials of representatives previously accredited and accepted. . . challenged by representatives of other states or where rival delegations present credentials it has been urged. . . that the appropriate organ of the United Nations has the right, if not the obligation to determine which credentials are to be accepted as valid.[39]

There are, however, complications in determining "which credentials are to be accepted as valid" by the organs of the United Nations. Two major problems remain to be solved. First, as Briggs fears, United Nations action on the issue of Chinese representation "may conceivably be regarded as intervention, contrary to the Charter in a matter essentially within the domestic jurisdiction of the Member state."[40] That is, since both governments of China insist — with the concurrence of the Soviet bloc — that the conflict between them is entirely within the domestic jurisdiction of China, a United Nations decision of this sort might conceivably be regarded as intervention in a continuing civil war. And, let us remember that Article 2, paragraph of the Charter states: "Nothing contained in the present Charter shall authorize the United Nations to intervene in matters which are essentially within the domestic jurisdiction of any state or shall require the Members to submit such matters to settlement under the present Charter."

As a result of a recent trend, within the United Nations themselves, toward an increasingly looser interpretation of the Charter, there have been instances of intervention — through majority resolutions in the General Assembly — in internal affairs of member states. So far most of such resolutions have dealt with various problems raised by devolution from "colonialism". Such resolutions have been resented by the governments concerned or, indeed, ignored entirely in cases where a country is striving to maintain its overseas colonial connections. Still, one may guess that a decision to replace the Nationalist by a Communist representative through a two-thirds vote in the General Assembly would be self-enforcing. And if the Nationalist government were to lose its claim to represent China at the United Nations, it could hardly retain physical possession of its seats in the various organs of that body. The decision could, however, be challenged on legal grounds. Such grounds are provided by the fact that the General Assembly resolutions have the force of recommendation only and each government has the option whether or not to follow such a recommendation. A great many General Assembly resolutions, their "moral force" notwithstanding, have been ignored by a multitude of countries. It is conceivable that representatives of the governments which have refused to recognize Communist China might choose to ignore its representatives in the organs of the United Nations.[41]

The second problem evolves from the peculiar position of

a permanent member of the Security Council. Since China is in this category, the problem of its representation in the UN becomes infinitely more complex. To begin with, there is a standing rule which provides that:

> As long as the Security Council does not decide that a person whom the Security Council has recognized as the representative of a member of the Council has lost this quality — because the government which had signed his credentials or of which he is a member has lost effective control over the territory and people concerned — this person is, within the meaning of the Charter, the representative of the Member state.[42]

But, if these provisions are taken literally, how can the Security Council decide the matter? We have already noted that Rule 17 of the Rules of Procedure says that "Any representative on the Security Council, to whose credentials objection has been made within the Security Council shall continue to sit with the same rights as other representatives until the Security Council has decided the matter." The representative of the Republic of China sitting in the Council possesses the right of veto. The veto is not applicable to procedural matters but as it has been indicated, the issue has ceased to be procedural. This point was stressed by Kelsen:

> It may be doubted whether the approval of credentials in this case is a decision on a merely procedural matter, for it implies the recognition on the part of the Security Council, and hence on the part of the United Nations, of a new government. But the view that it is a decision on a nonprocedural matter leads to the absurd consequence that the person still acting as a representative of the Member Council, may prevent the approval of the credentials signed by the new government by exercising the veto right of the permanent member.[43]

It is possible that decision to expel the representative of the Republic of China from the Security Council might be declared valid if the representatives of the United States, United Kingdom and France elect not to exercise their right of veto (that is, to abstain from voting) and if seven members vote in favor. Greene may be correct in asserting that "it is extremely doubtful that the

Nationalists can hold their seat in the Security Council by resorting to the veto without American backing."[44] Yet, if in the event of a showdown, the Nationalist representative should decide to contest the matter — and, after all, what would he, or his government, stand to lose by so doing? — this method of expelling him besides causing a universal scandal would amount, *ipso facto,* to an arbitrary revision of the Charter of the United Nations — a step likely to have far-reaching legal and political repercussions.

NEW TRENDS IN THE UNITED NATIONS

With the passage of time, initial bitterness over the issue of Chinese representation in the United Nations has decreased substantially and a majority of member states have seemed to resign themselves to following the United States' lead. At the beginning of each new session, the General Assembly has continued to vote to postpone consideration of the issue — "for the duration of the session." However, since the end of the Korean War certain international developments have taken place which put this issue into a new perspective.

For one thing, since the middle 50's, the Soviet Union has gained considerably in international respectability. This has not been simply the result of the prestige dividend gained by its scientific-technological progress in nuclear weapons and rocketry; important also is its adoption of a seemingly less doctrinaire attitude towards international relations. The resort to bloodshed, as in Korea and Indochina, apparently ended. The "summit" meeting in Geneva in the summer of 1955 — the first meeting, since the beginning of the Cold War between the heads of the American, British and French governments, and Soviet leaders — accomplished little. Nevertheless, it helped somewhat to dispel the established image of communist intransigence and aggressiveness. The old image fully reappeared in the crushing of the Hungarian uprising of 1956, and in the Chinese suppression of Tibet in 1959, but there has been a tendency in the West, whether correct or not, to treat these as aberrations. Whether this trend can withstand the impact of Soviet behavior in and action toward the U.N., or of the now renewed crisis over Berlin remains to be seen. At least on one occasion — during the Suez crisis — the United States joined the Soviet Union in denouncing Great Britain and France. On another, the object of Soviet-American joint denunciations turned out to be Portugal, a U.S. NATO ally.

A second element of change has been the growth of the "neutralist" group in the United Nations. Instead of a dozen countries which avoid permanent alignment with either side in the Cold War — as at the time of the Korean War — there are now over 40 countries which may be placed in this category. At least on issues relating to "colonialism," they have tended to vote as a bloc. Some of them, like Ghana, Guinea, Mali, the United Arab Republic and a few others have also shown a disposition often to support the communist bloc on general issues related to the Cold War. The days when the Soviets were in a pitiful minority on almost every question coming to a vote in the General Assembly are past.

Soviet progress in the military field gave rise to a fear of another world war. The uncertainties arising from thermo-nuclear deadlock constitute a thrid, psycho-social factor of change on the international scene. Offering an "answer" which capitalizes on the doubts of many individuals, the pacifist movement has again become an important factor in exerting pressure on many governments which up till now have supported a more or less firmly anti-communist position. The American nuclear deterrent no longer seems to be a sufficient guarantee against Soviet attack. Soviet atomic blackmail from the mid-1950's onward, began to pay off and resulting demands for arms-control and disarmament have led to a search for a *modus vivendi* with the communist governments.

In the light of these developments, renewal of debate over Chinese representation in the United Nations was unavoidable. Though pressures from individual member states for reconsideration of the issue are only slightly more noticeable than before and though few countries have defected from the American-led majority which continues to oppose the seating of Communist China, the numerical "score-card" on the issue has indeed changed.

VOTING IN THE GENERAL ASSEMBLY ON POSTPONEMENT OF THE DISCUSSION OF THE ISSUE OF CHINESE REPRESENTATION

Session	Voted for postponement	Voted against postponement	Percentage of votes "for"	Abstained	Total membership
6th (1951)	37	11	77	4	60
7th (1952)	42	7	85	11	60
8th (1953)	44	10	81	2	60
9th (1954)	43	11	79	6	60
10th (1955)	42	12	77	6	60
11th (1956)	47	24	66	8	79
12th (1957)	47	27	63	7	82
13th (1958)	44	28	61	9	81
14th (1959)	44	29	60	4	82
15th (1960)	42	34	56	22	99

The data extracted from Annual Reports of the Secretary-General to the General Assembly

However, a minority of 34 votes — even less, if one takes into account probable abstentions — would suffice to prevent the seating of Communist China in the United Nations. Nobody has yet suggested that the opposition could not rally this minimum voting support. Nor has the possibility been ruled out that this trend in voting might level off at some future date. In fact, as we shall see later, there are possibilities of even reversing the trend. Nevertheless, the mere prospect that the West, for once, might not command a majority produces in some circles a fatalistic mood of defeat even before the battle starts. This defeatism has manifested itself in many ways: in the talk of "inevitability" of the Western loss of its position; in efforts to rationalize the Chinese Communist entry into the United Nations as advantageous from the Western point of view; and in blaming the United States "inflexibility" in dealing with the issue, — a stand which, presumably, has in itself brought about the lamentable situation in which the West finds itself with regard to China. For example, Inis Claude wrote (in 1956):

In contrast with the League, which lost little time in emptying its comparable provisions of their moral content, the United Nations has purported to take seriously its ethical standards to new members. . . . Circumstances and political interests have decreed that the United States should become the foremost exponent of the view that the United Nations should serve as a Moral Accreditation Agency. . . . This is not an unfamiliar or inappropriate role for the United States, with its tradition of regarding moral aspiration and moral indignation as instruments of foreign policy. . . . Rejoicing in this role, the United States has filled the international air with talk about preserving the moral integrity of the United Nations, standing firm against iniquitious attempts of governments to "shoot their way into the United Nations" or to gain admission by blackmail.[45]

In line with a contemporary trend among both publicists and political scientists, accusations of the excessive moralizing on the part of the United States have been many; yet, it is characteristic that at least some exponents of the "realistic" and "United Nations point of view" have themselves indulged in moralizing whenever this suits their purpose. As Hans J. Morgenthau observes, many of them expect the United Nations

to initiate a kind of international politics in which nations would pool their power for common purposes rather than pit them against each other in competition. This expectation was supported both by the spirit and the letter of the Charter of the United Nations and by the climate of opinion prevailing at the end of the Second World War. The Charter predicates the successful operations of the United Nations upon the continuing unity of the great powers, working in harmony within the framework of the Charter. The Charter assumes that harmony, it cannot create it. . . . When that initial hope of a dawning millenium has been disappointed, it was replaced by another hope, equally utopian, that the United Nations could establish peace between East and West. . . . It was widely believed that a dispute, by being put on the agenda of an agency of the United Nations, would somehow lose its sting and become susceptible to a peaceful settlement which could not be otherwise obtained, . . . as though there were in the United Nations a healing power which need only be invoked to make itself prevail.[46]

American skepticism as to the "healing power" of the United Nations has been often condemned. At the same time, the defenders of the "United Nations interests" realize that without American support the United Nations has no chance to fulfill its functions. In order to increase this support, they seek to identify the "United Nations interests" with those of the United States, and to present this as both realism and idealism. Greene says:

> The United Nations serves as a universal conscience of sorts, giving all security issues a global perspective. Since the Soviet bloc operates on a global front. . . it can be argued that the United Nations must provide a counter-motivation and commitment which makes any assault the concern of all members. Otherwise, the tendency. . . to ignore unpleasant events in distant lands becomes too tempting. The United States possesses the power and strategic geographic location to take effective action in scattered areas vulnerable to aggressions; hence the United Nations collective security arrangement coincides with basic American policy.[47]

Such conclusions are, of course, bitterly denounced by the communists and are increasingly opposed by the "neutralists". Flattering as they may sound to the United States, such ideas thus far have not been able to induce this nation to tie its foreign policy to the United Nations — although President Kennedy has called the UN the "last, best hope for peace." And, in particular, simple assertion of the identity of American interests with those of the United Nations has not produced a change in the American position on the issue of Chinese representation. Nor — after ten years without Communist China in the world organization — would it seem that many have been, or are likely to be convinced by repetition of the argument, that the Peking regime must be seated simply by virtue of its "effective control" over most of China. Thus, those who advocate such representation find it necessary to introduce new arguments, political rather than formal in nature, in the attempt to convince the United States that it stands to gain, rather than lose, from a reversal of its position on this issue. Such arguments are many: some stress the opportunity to please those Afro-Asians who are unhappy over the American "inflexibility", others the advantages of "universal" composition of the United Nations as distinct from "selective", others the possible beneficial or "taming" effects on Communist China of United Nations membership. The list of arguments could be extended even further.

A. Doak Barnett in attempting to assess these points, says:

> The seating of Peking would doubtless add somewhat to the influence of the Communist bloc in the United Nations; . . . it might bolster the Communists' attempts to manipulate the Asian-African bloc. [But] conceivably, the non-Communist nations in the Asian-African group might be able to exert certain influence upon Chinese Communist policies, as well as the reverse. . . . If seated in the United Nations [Communist China] might be somewhat more influenced than at present by the restraints of world opinion and might feel compelled to give more deference to the United Nations Charter and resolutions.[48]

The United States is again and again warned not to use the power of veto in the Security Council for the purpose of blocking the entry of the Chinese Communist representative, for this "would risk seriously straining or splitting the organization and would almost certainly have divisive effects tending to weaken rather than strengthen the entire non-Communist position.[49]

Another recurrent argument is that the trend toward universality in the United Nations is irresistible and that this trend, in itself, is beneficial. The point, for example, is expounded by Inis Claude who writes:

> For the realization of the purposes of the United Nations as originally formulated, it is clear that the rule of essentiality coincides approximately with the principle of universality. . . . If the United Nations is to serve as the focal point for efforts to settle the disputes, moderate the attitudes, solve the problems, and eliminate the conditions which make for war and insecurity, its ranks should be as wide as possible. A highly selective membership is obviously inappropriate.[50]

These lines were written after the first big "package deal" of 1955, when of the then existing governments, all but Communist China, Outer Mongolia, Switzerland, the two Germanys, the two Koreas and the two Vietnams were admitted to the United Nations. To call that membership "highly selective" (especially since no

100

one as yet had advocated admission of the last six governments) is, of course, preposterous. It may mean only one thing: that, apparently, it is the presence of Communist China that is the in-dispensable criterion proposed by some advocates of "universality".

No more convincing, in view of the Soviet behavior is the argument that with Communist China in, the United Nations would be in a better position "to settle the disputes, moderate the attitudes, solve the problems, and eliminate the conditions which make for war and insecurity." Still weaker is the argument which deals with the promise of disarmament:

> The UN is a world forum in which. . . we ought to insist that membership should be regarded as a mandatory obligation of all states. . . . It is not possible to adopt such a view. . . until the problem of Communist Chinese representation is settled, an event that will probably take place not by the resolution. . . but because at some future moment progress in the field of disarmament. . . cannot be institutionalized without the participation of a country covering a significant portion of the earth's physi-cal surface and containing a quarter of its inhabitants.[51]

Similar sentiments have been voiced by Adlai E. Stevenson:

> It is clear that no general control of disarmament has any value unless it includes China, and it is difficult to see how China can accept international control when it is not, formally, a member of international society. Moreover, as a member of the United Nations, Communist China. . . would be more accountable to world opinion than as an outcast.[52]

Disarmament, i.e. the play on universal fear of another major war, seems to be one of the highest trump cards played so far by the advocates of the seating of Communist China in the United Nations. How membership in the United Nations is going to induce militant regimes to agree to disarm has not yet been shown by anyone. Claude, in fact, privately admits that bringing up the dis-armament issue in the United Nations tends to make its solution much more difficult.[53] Nevertheless, some authors insist that the Peking regime ought to occupy the place of China in the United Nations as an encouragement toward better behavior, particularly if the interminable East-West talks on disarmament begin to yield any practical results.[54]

All these arguments are by no means limited to individual writers: similar views have been expressed in many "neutralist" and in some Western capitals, especially in places where pacifist pressures make themselves felt or where there is a willingness to scrap, for the sake of modern day "realism", the so-called "abstract" values. On the other hand, however, the case for seating Communist China in the United Nations stripped of all pretenses, appears to make little, if any, sense from the Western point of view.

The only indisputable interest in membership for Communist China is that of the Soviet Union. Granted that China is not just another satellite, and that thus the presence of the Chinese Communists would somewhat complicate the Soviet task of presenting a united front of communist countries in the United Nations, the strategic advantages of such membership from the communist point of view are immeasurable. Quite unperturbed by speculations on the so-called Sino-Soviet rift, the Soviet government, therefore, has consistently and vociferously demanded the expulsion of the Chinese Nationalists and their replacement by the Chinese Communists in all organs of the United Nations. In his address to the General Assembly on September 18, 1959, Khrushchev said:

> It is inconceivable that anyone could earnestly think that a stable and reliable solution of major world problems could be achieved without the participation of the Great People's China, which is approaching its glorious tenth anniversary. . . . Why then must China be represented in the United Nations by the corpse of reactionary China, that is by the Chiang Kai-shek clique?[55]

Khrushchev's advocacy of the seating of the Peking regime in the United Nations took even more forceful, if less coherent form a year later in his famous shoe-banging speech during the fifteenth session of the General Assembly. One would have to be unusually credulous, in view of this performance, to think that in the depths of his heart Khrushchev, by some strange logic, hoped that his efforts to bring the Chinese Communists into the councils of the United Nations would be defeated.

The views of Secretary-General Dag Hammarskjold on this

subject are unknown. It may be surmised that initially he might have favored Peking's presence in the organization. However, since the ill-fated attempt of Trygve Lie to bring Communist China in on strictly formal grounds, the office of the Secretary-General has avoided taking any stand on the issue. Without much chance for success, it would be unwise to alienate Nationalist China which, after all, occupies a permanent seat in the Security Council and is able, should it choose, to veto measures favored by the Secretariat. There are grounds to suspect, however, that in recent years the harsh realities of United Nations' institutional life in a world split by global conflicts has brought disappointment to at least some who had, at one time, been enthusiastic about the prospect of representation for Communist China. One may even venture to guess that Hammarskjold's natural preoccupation with the preservation of the United Nations as a working body has led him to conclude that it is better to put up with the imperfection of having one "great outsider" than risk having another first-class trouble-maker in the very precincts of the United Nations.

REALITIES OF THE UNITED NATIONS

As one reviews the controversy over Chinese representation it is difficult to escape the impression that many of those who favor the seating of Communist China in the United Nations do not particularly identify themselves with the West in the Cold War. At the very least, they appear to seek some middle ground between two opposing camps. More often, they live in a world of their own, the image of which they project into the United Nations. There, the voice of Yemen, or Upper Volta, or Cambodia, registers as loudly as that of a great power, and the unfolding drama manifests itself in often meaningless and inconsequential resolutions carried sometimes by coincidental majorities of nations which often work at cross purposes, or for no clearly understood common purpose at all. The illusionists' thinking is often distorted by their image of the United Nations as a kind of town meeting which is a true reflection of the world of today, save for the absence of Communist China and few other countries. (The lack of representation of these other countries, for some reason, is not a matter of special concern to "universalists", although these states' combined power in terms of population, economic, political and military factors is no smaller than that of Communist China.)

Even while expounding their familiarities with the "realities" of today's United Nations, the proponents of the Chinese Communists' entry tend to underestimate unmistakable signs of that organization's potential engulfment by the Cold War, an engulfment which has recently spread to areas and issues not previously affected by the East-West struggle. In other words, many of them see the United Nations not as it is but as they would imagine it to be, or as a prototype of some sort of world government in which various regions and political trends are justly represented and everybody pursues the common good. Many are reluctant to recognize that clashing with their image of "one world" is the reality of "civil war" between the Western and communist camps. Their only worry is that a particular region — China — is "underrepresented" and they insist on bringing it in even if it would mean further intensification of this "civil war" and an accession of power on that side of the barricades which threatens to destroy the existing world structure, including the United Nations itself.

Following from these images, it is characteristic of some noncommunist champions of the seating of the Peking regime that they see the United Nations as turning into a "neutralist" organization of which the mainspring is an alliance of those small and so-called non-aligned nations who represent the largest single "group" in the General Assembly. In their eyes, this group may act as a kind of "third force" in the East-West struggle, a powerful buffer which alone can safeguard the hope of humanity and which, by some magic, can prevent an ultimate collision between the power-drunk Goliaths. Therefore, they attach utmost importance to, indeed pin their hopes upon, the "unity" of a conglomeration of nations whose attitude to global problems has been anything but homogeneous and who have united, most of the time, only around a strictly negative issue, that of "anti-colonialism".

Because the proponents of the "United Nations point of view" imagine this group to be a great force *per se*, they are inclined to underestimate the increasingly obvious fact that these "neutral" countries, still smarting over their colonial past, have proven, in too many cases, to be easily susceptible to Soviet bait. Their erstwhile spokesman, India, could not compete with the Soviet Union in the violence of her denunciations of "colonialism". Neither could she offer much in the way of material inducements toward preservation of the chastity of the "Third Force". Communist inroads into new areas have usually been spearheaded by the lure of arms (at cut-rate prices), by offers of free "education" in Moscow or Prague, and by economic and technical assistance to the chosen few. And although aid coming to new countries from the West has been many times larger, it has somehow little affected the political-psychological climate in underdeveloped areas. For it has been easy to find cynics who charge that the West has been acting out of strictly selfish considerations, that in any event, it has to atone for previous guilt, and, in addition, that it seemed to be quite willing to be pushed around. To be sure, the more sophisticated leaders of the noncommitted world do suspect that the Soviet motives are not exactly pure, but, wooed by both sides and thinking and caring little about the ideals upon which the world organization was founded, they take whatever comes their way and happily enjoy their sudden position of importance in the United Nations.

With a closer look at the foreign policies of the presumably neutral countries the myth of the "Third Force" vanishes without a trace. (The fact that many of them suppress the communists domestically, while joining the forces of communism internationally, need not confuse us.) First, we notice that the World of the Neutral is by no means static. Second, that during the last decade the trends in it have been distinctly unfavorable to the West. Even within the West itself — if by the "west" we mean the nations belonging to the North Atlantic Treaty organization — there have been considerable frictions, while other regional blocs originated by the West — like CENTO and SEATO — are close to a breaking point. But once we enter the so-called non-aligned world we discover a much more complex picture than is usually imagined. In order to see it, it is sufficient to break the "neutral" nations into several groups according to their position between the two major camps. Such a breakdown is necessarily arbitrary but it helps to illustrate the point.

RELATIVE POSITIONS OF NON-ALIGNED NATIONS
(Summer 1961)

"West": the NATO group.

Pro-Western: Spain, Iran*, Pakistan, Thailand, South Vietnam, the Philippines, Republic of China, South Korea, Japan†, Australia, New Zealand, most of Latin America‡.

Pro-Western "neutrals": Sweden, Switzerland, Austria, most of the former French Africa, Israel, Jordan, Malaya.

Anti-Communist "neutrals": Tunisia, Libya, Lebanon, Saudi Arabia, Union of South Africa, the Congo (Leopoldville), Haiti, Dominican Republic, Cyprus, Vatican, Laos☆.

Anti-Western "neutrals": Ethopia, most of the former British Africa, Iraq, India, Nepal, Cambodia.

Communist-oriented "neutrals": Finland, Morocco, Ghana, Somalia, Yemen, Afganistan, Burma, Indonesia, Ceylon.

Communist-oriented: Guinea, Mali, Cuba, U.A.R., Yugoslavia★.

Communist: the Soviet Union, Poland, Czechoslovakia, Hungary, Roumania, Bulgaria, Albania, East Germany, Communist China, Outer Mongolia, North Vietnam, North Korea.

Notes: *An internal upheaval in Iran which would favor the communists is a distinct possibility.
†There is a strong "neutralist" and pacifist sentiment developing in Japan which might cause that country's shift into the next category.
‡"Neutralist" tendencies are developing in Brazil and, to a lesser extent, in some other Latin-American countries.
☆Laos is likely to end-up in the "communist-oriented" group.
★A maverick in the communist bloc, Yugoslavia votes consistently with the Soviets in the United Nations, otherwise tries to ally itself with the communist-oriented nations with certain claim to neutrality.

It should be pointed out that since Yugoslavia's break with the Soviets in 1948 there have been no material shifts favoring the West, with the possible exception of Iraq — where a pro-communist trend has been temporarily arrested — and that of India where the Chinese Communists' incursions along the northern frontier have generated enough anti-communist sentiment to force the Indian government to take a more tolerable attitude toward the West.

It is important to note that the way the "neutrals" orient their foreign policies has little to do with their internal socio-political structure; cultural, religious and economic factors play a more significant role. More important, however, is the intensity of anti-Western emotions in former colonial areas — those which form the basis of modern nationalism. In taking positions on various "cold war" issues many governments are often guided not by rational considerations but by a desire to stress their anti-Western posture.

The way the "neutrals" cast their vote in the General Assembly on the Chinese representation issue reflects the current trends better than the balloting on any other issue. It is only in rare cases that a "neutral" country votes against the West out of a deep conviction that Communist China has to be seated in the United Nations as a matter of principle. Much more often, they vote against the West either out of spite, in order to assert their independence, or because they had committed themselves by an early recognition of the Peking government in pre-Korean days, or out of the hope to profit by trading with mainland China, or, finally, because of the growing belief that the communists hold the cards and that Soviet gratitude has to be sought. Since the West has made only feeble attempts to use the United Nations as an instrument to uphold basically Western concepts and interests,[56] the anti-Western trend has been gaining momentum in recent years; in all, it creates an extremely fluid situation, used to the fullest by the communist bloc. This fluidity and resulting advantage to the communist bloc, can only increase if Communist China is seated in the United Nations.

*   *   *

Let us assume that, as a result of a possible shift in the American position, combined with other developments, the representatives of Communist China take over China's place in the United Nations. In such a case what will be the likely consequences? Let us consider three of them.

First, the elevation of Communist China to a role as one of the guardians of international peace and security in the Security Council would automatically increase the dangers to the independence of countries like South Korea, the Philippines, South Vietnam, Laos, Malaya, or Thailand. Their shaky regimes would feel abandoned and might well fall easy prey to pressures emanating from the most powerful nation of the region, even if the Chinese Communists did not resort to overt aggression. The pro-Western governments of these countries might, for a short time, give place to "neutralist" ones as a stage before landing in the communist camp. The United Nations, quite clearly, could do nothing to prevent this from happening. In other words, one more group of nations would lose their independence, and Communist China would acquire a belt of satellites in the Soviet fashion.

There is also, of course, the problem of Taiwan. It can hardly be doubted that the "two Chinas" concept will not work in the United Nations. There would be no sane reason for the Peking government to abandon its claim to sovereignty over Taiwan exactly at the very time when its right to represent China in the United Nations was favored by more countries than ever before. The promoters of the so-called "United Nations point of view" have displayed a remarkable callousness towards the fate of smaller nations, especially if these nations happen to suffer from the strong-arm policies of the communist powers. According to their scale of values, Taiwan or other small countries, are not worth much. If these views prevail, the present representatives of the Republic of China would be evicted from the United Nations — or would walk out of it — much to the satisfaction of the communist bloc. Could such a scandalous act possibly help the United Nations? What small and independent nation would be able to feel sure that it would not, in turn, at some future date, become a victim of such accommodation? Will the betrayals of the '30s (Ethopia, Czechoslovakia), which had such disastrous consequences, be repeated again?

There is one additional danger. If the United States, as a result of accepting some form of United Nations protection for Taiwan, backs out of its own commitment to defend Taiwan, the threat of war in the Far East would increase sharply: the Peking government, encouraged by its success in the United Nations, might decide to make good on its promise of long standing and "liberate" Taiwan from the "Chiang Kai-shek clique." In such a case the United States would almost automatically become involved in the conflict under United Nations auspices.

Finally there is the problem of the United Nations itself.

Its image has already changed considerably. As "neutrals" become increasingly dominant in its deliberations, many Europeans tend to question its usefulness. Stanley Evans, former member of Parliament and a Laborite, writing in *The New York Times* on June 11, 1961, suggests that "Any institution that accords the same power of decision to tribal chiefs as to the representatives of the United States and Russia is utopian to the point of lunacy." And William J. Hamilton, a long-time *New York Times* observer of the United Nations scene wrote in his newspaper in April, 1961:

> If the Soviet Union (and Communist China when it is admitted) should succeed in the attempt to get control of the anti-colonial and neutralist forces in the organization, a very disagreeable situation will develop for the West. It is not outside the range of possibility that our Western European Allies will eventually get so irritated that they will leave the United Nations and set up their own regional organization.

But even before such a development could take place, the very appearance of Communist China would mean the organization's further shift away from the predominantly Western image in which it was cast in 1945. There is only one direction the United Nations could then take, for the weakening of the West would mean strengthening of the communist positions. In anticipation of this, more and more people are beginning to argue that:

> The United Nations should reduce its commitments in the field [of securing international peace] and point to the record of the League of Nations, whose success was most striking in non-security matters. The Cold War has created mutually hostile camps in the United Nations, a condition inimical to the successful operation of collective security, where all are required to join together against an isolated aggressor.[57]

This is a likely course anyway. After it became evident that the United Nations Congo operation had greatly overtaxed the organization's effective resources, the great powers have increasingly showed a disposition to bypass the United Nations altogether whenever their vital interests have been involved: in the cease-fire arrangements in Laos and in the Geneva discussions on political settlement in that country, in exchanges over the Berlin crisis, in disarmament talks. After the new administration was installed in Washington, the United States has been reluctant to utilize the United Nations forum even for propaganda purposes. The communist bloc, by its attacks on Hammarskjold and its demands of replacing the Secretary-General's office by a "triumvirate" is undermining the organization's role in world affairs even more. Such a degradation of the United Nations has been perhaps unavoidable and it might be that the sooner its limitations in dealing with political and military conflicts are realized, the better. After all, the United Nations, as an organization working successfully in the area of technical and economic assistance, studiously avoiding any involvement in big or small conflicts of power and ideology, is obviously preferable, from a Western point of view, to its becoming a tool in the hands of disproportionately vocal "neutrals", or of the communist bloc.

ALTERNATIVES

One logical alternative to the appearance of Communist China in the United Nations is, of course, to continue to keep it out. As of late, suggestions have been coming from around the United Nations headquarters that this course is doomed. It has been argued that the question is no longer whether Communist China *should* be seated in the United Nations but rather in what form the seating *will* take place, that is whether the communists take the seats in both the Security Council and the General Assembly, along with other organs of the organization, or some form of the "two Chinas" solution could be worked out according to which the "Taiwan regime" would retain a seat in the General Assembly as a minor power. Urban Whitaker, in his unpublished research memorandum, points out the growing willingness on the part of some formerly Western-oriented "neutrals" "to place their own convictions on the subject above their 'sense of attachment' to the United States." He explains this phenonmenon by the rapid growth of the United

Nations and by the change in administration in Washington: "The former makes independent voting easier by increasing the number who try it. The latter makes it easier by decreasing the penalties for independence. Whether the new administration is, in fact, any more willing than the old to tolerate independence among its allies is less important that the widespread *feeling* that this is true."

This brings us to a conclusion that a possibility of keeping Communist China out hinges, to a large extent, on the degree of the United States determination to follow the old "negative" policy on this issue. As a major world power and a chief contributor to various United Nations operations and projects, it is in a position to subdue the voices of those in and around the Secretariat who claim to represent the "United Nations point of view". The United States can also influence its numerous allies and those countries which depend heavily upon American aid and good-will. The effectiveness of American diplomacy in the United Nations has, for a number of years, been substandard. Much has been taken for granted, little has been done to nail down real support. For any decline in support in the General Assembly, ephemeral as this support is, the United States has itself to blame.

During the 1960 session of the Assembly 42 countries voted against considering the Chinese representation issue, 34 voted for it, while 22 abstained. The line-up was irregular and did not always reflect the individual country's attitude toward Communist China. Let us consider the groupings.

A. Nations which favor a discussion of the issue and which have recognized Communist China (Byleorussia and the Ukraine are included in this grouping although they maintain no diplomatic relations with any country.) :

Afghanistan	Finland	Norway
Albania	Ghana	Poland
Bulgaria	Guinea	Roumania
Burma	Hungary	Sudan
Byelorussia	India	Sweden
Cambodia	Indonesia	Ukraine
Ceylon	Iraq	U.S.S.R.
Cuba	Mali	U.A.R.
Czechoslovakia	Morocco	Yemen
Denmark	Nepal	Yugoslavia

B. Nations which favor a discussion of the issue but which do not recognize either the Rupublic of China or the Peking regime:

Ethiopia   Ireland   Nigeria

C. Nations which both favor discussion and recognize the Republic of China: Senegal

D. Nations which abstained from voting but which recognize the Peking regime (Somalia and Upper Volta recognized Peking after the vote was cast.):

Israel   Somalia   Upper Volta

E. Nations which abstained and which recognize neither:

Austria   Ivory Coast
Central African Republic   Malaya
Chad   Nigeria
Dahomey   Tunisia
Iceland

F. Nations which abstained but which recognize the Republic of China:

Cameroon   Laos   Portugal
Congo (Brazzaville)   Libya   Saudi Arabia
Cyprus   Malagasy   Togo
Gabon

G. Nations which voted against a discussion but which recognize the Peking regime:

Netherlands   Pakistan   United Kingdom

H. Nations which voted against a discussion and which recognize the Republic of China:

Argentina	Greece	Nicaragua
Australia	Guatemala	Panama
Belgium	Haiti	Paraguay
Bolivia	Honduras	Peru
Brazil	Iran	Philippines
Canada	Italy	Spain
Chile	Japan	Thailand
Colombia	Jordan	Turkey
Costa Rica	Lebanon	Union of South Africa
Dominican Republic	Liberia	United States
Ecuador	Luxembourg	Uruguay
El Salvador	Mexico	Venezuela
France	New Zealand	(Republic of China)

112

The Congo (Leopoldville) which recognized the Republic of China was admitted to the United Nations after the voting.

There are several conclusions that can be drawn from the 1960 vote on this issue.

1. Out of 36 member nations which, as of the summer of 1961, have recognized Communist China, thirty favored a discussion of the Chinese representation, three were against and three abstained.

2. Out of 50 member nations which recognized the Republic of China 38 were against a discussion, 10 abstained, one voted for, and one did not vote.

3. Those who abstained from voting are either new African nations which belong to the French community, or the more pro-Western Arab nations, or countries like Cyprus, Portugal, Austria, Iceland, Israel, Malaya, and Laos which, for various reasons either choose non-alignment with either of the main groups, or have a vested interest in keeping Communist China out but dare not say so.

4. Not a single predominantly Catholic nation outside of the communist bloc favors the seating of Communist China, although Ireland wants the issue to be discussed.

5. The "French" African States, with the exception of communist-oriented Mali, Guinea and Upper Volta, tend to recognize the Republic of China.

6. The African and Asian members of the Commonwealth tend to recognize the Peking regime.

7. The Arab League countries are split on the issue, with U.A.R., Morocco, Sudan, Iraq and Yemen voting alongside the Soviet Union.

A projection of this 1960-1961 picture into the future reveals a possibility of further defections from the American-led group. The United Kingdom, Brazil and Pakistan are likely to favor a discussion of the issue. If the United States position softens further, it is estimated that the Soviet-led bloc might gain a total of from five to eight votes. On the other hand, it is possible that the African states of the French community, alarmed more than the others by communist tactics in the Congo and the communist foothold in Guinea and Mali, would move closer to the United States.

It is not at all certain, moreover, that those who would vote in favor of *discussion* of the issue would necessarily vote in favor of *seating* the Chinese Communists. In this connection, the composition of the General (Credentials) Committee of the General Assembly would play an important role. During the 15th session out of its 13 members only four were known to favor a discussion (plus its chairman, the President of the General Assembly). As long as the Committee, by a simple majority decision, recommends a postponement, a *two-thirds majority* in the General Assembly is needed to *upset* its recommendation (a *simple* majority is enough to *approve* it.) Regardless, however, of whether a discussion of Chinese representation takes place or not — and there are indications that even the United States might favor such a discussion at the next session, — the actual issue of which government should have the seat of China in the United Nations must be decided in the Assembly by a two-thirds majority. Short of a total collapse of the American position in the world, the chances for the opposition to gather that majority are nil.

If a resolution is submitted recommending the expulsion of the Republic of China from the United Nations, as demanded by Communist China, no more than a third of the members is likely to vote for it. A "two Chinas" proposal would not get more than a half, with the communist bloc firmly opposing. To sum up, it can easily be shown that predictions of the "inevitability" of Communist China's entry into the United Nations are based on wishful thinking more than on anything else. So far as one can see, the United States would always be able to gather the one-third of the votes necessary to keep Communist China out.

The picture is even more clear in the present Security Council. Of the six non-permanent members, only Ceylon and U.A.R. favor the admission of Communist China. Chile, Ecuador, Liberia, and Turkey are opposed. There is a possibility that for propaganda and other reasons the United States may declare that it considers the issue to be a procedural one and would not, therefore, insist on its right to use veto. In such a case, France and the Republic of China are likely to do the same. But even a procedural question, to be decided, needs seven votes in favor. With Great Britain and the Soviet Union voting in favor of seating Communist China, there would still be only four affirmative votes cast.

Of course, the terms of Ceylon, Ecuador and Turkey expire in 1961, that of the other non-permanent members in 1962, but it is highly improbable that one day five out of any six likely non-permanent members would vote against the United States. At any rate it is the legitimate function of Western diplomacy to see to it that the Security Council is not packed with countries which tend to vote with the Soviet Union on major issues.

Needless to say, in itself, successful action in preventing the Peking regime from taking China's seat in the United Nations is not a satisfactory solution of the problem. The disadvantages of the absence of Communist China in many organs of the United Nations are obvious. These disadvantages, however, cannot outweigh the advantage of keeping a major international trouble-maker out. The only solution at present acceptable to the majority of non-communist nations, that of "two Chinas", is ruled out by Peking's intransigence, intransigence supported by the Soviet Union. Thus, the whole issue becomes rather academic. There are many problems in the international life of our times which defy solution and this is clearly one of them. It would be folly to risk further upsetting the United Nations, which is already in a precarious position, by admitting Communist China in a vague hope that somehow things will take care of themselves. Therefore, we find ourselves repeating, at the end of our investigation, the maxim that "politics, or the art of politics, especially international politics, consists of choosing between or among various different evils."

* * *

Universality of membership one day might be accepted by the United Nations as one of the principles of the organization. It could be done either by a formal revision of the Charter or as a part of the continuous *de facto* modernization of its image through resolutions, "package deals", or by a tacit consent of a simple, or qualified, majority. An all-embracing United Nations may, or may not, function better than the old one. But unless and until the principle of universality of membership is accepted by the world organization, there is little merit in using it as an argument for the seating of Communist China.

Any major change in the United Nations make-up must be acceptable to the West in general and to the United States in particular. To effect such a change against the will of the West would do the United Nations no good, for technical majorities can be, and often are, quite meaningless. Resolutions passed by the General Assembly and other organs of the United Nations can have — and sometimes do have — destructive consequences. If there is a path towards an accommodation between the East and the West and between the developed North and the South of the newly emerged nations, it does not lead through the seating of Communist China on its own terms — in other words, not through yielding to the pressures inimical to the principles of the United Nations Charter and to the interests of the Western Nations.

NEW TRENDS IN THE UNITED STATES

As of the summer of 1961, the United States remains the main obstacle to Communist China's entry into the United Nations. Until the very last days of the Eisenhower administration, the government remained adamantly opposed to such a move and succeeded in persuading some of its reluctant allies to maintain a united front whenever the Soviet Union or India renewed their attacks on the American position.

In the United States, demands for reconsideration of the policy toward China have been infrequent; such demands as do appear, have been limited to a rather small group of writers on international law and relations and to some politicians of liberal persuasion. Since, in the public mind, the question of Chinese representation in the United Nations has been inextricably linked to the question of recognition of the Peking government — a bitter pill the swallowing of which the majority of the American electorate has continued to resist — these critics have failed to develop any significant following.

Nevertheless, in the years following the Korean War there has been a marked decline in the bitterness of the public attitude toward Communist China. With the passing of John Foster Dulles, and the disappearance from the Senate in 1958 of its leading spokesman for an uncompromising policy toward communism, William F. Knowland, the supporters of the position of holding the present line lost their most prominent leaders. There was no one of stature left on the political scene who was willing to go on record as favoring United States withdrawal from the United Nations should the Chinese Communists be seated.[58] Popular sentiment supporting such a move has also declined.

From a strictly American point of view, the most telling argument against giving the Peking regime the stature and prestige of a major power occupying a permanent seat in the Security Council has been that such a step would endanger the independence of a number of nations which compose the strategic alliances that the United States has built up in Asia.

Yet, the obvious abnormality of Sino-American relations has led many writers to look for at least a partial modification of the American policy toward China, which, while preserving a general posture of containment, would make room for some sort of a *rapprochement* with the Mao Tse-tung regime and some reduction of tensions between the two countries. This search for a new stance has not been fruitful. All it has produced, so far, is a number of proposals which boil down to the so-called "two Chinas" solution. As early as 1955, Arthur H. Dean suggested recognition of Communist China and its admission as a new member of the United Nations, while maintaining relations with the Republic of China (on Taiwan) and supporting its position as a permanent member in the Security Council.[59] The same year, Quincy Wright offered a modified version of the original Trygve Lie proposal, suggesting that:

> The United States is free to recognize Formosa and the Pescadores as an independent state under the Nationalist government. . . provided free and fair elections indicate that an independent state of Formosa under the Nationalist government conforms to the wishes of the inhabitants.[60]

Two years later Wright repeated this proposal, adding that a "two Chinas" solution would strengthen the United Nations, provided that the communists were given China's permanent seat in the Security Council.[61]

117

The "two Chinas" solution has been rejected in no uncertain terms by both Peking and Taipei. The United States government, at least under the Eisenhower administration, felt that it owed a measure of loyalty to its ally, Nationalist China, and that the price of mollifying the Chinese Communists without prior modification of their anti-American posture would be prohibitive. Still, variations of the "two Chinas" proposal keep cropping up and, with the passage of time, take forms increasingly more favorable to the communists. The majority of these critics are agreed that Peking has an indisputable right to represent China in all organs of the United Nations. Taiwan, in their view, could be considered for admission as a new member, as a part of some kind of a "package deal." The main argument in favor of such a deal has a distinctly fatalistic ring, for it consists of the assertion that Communist China is bound to be brought in, sooner or later. Thus, Chester Bowles wrote in 1958:

> Pressure in the United Nations for seating Communist China in place of Nationalist China is likely to grow during the next few years. If a British Labor government comes into office in 1960, it is almost certain to reverse the present position of the United Kingdom on this issue and other delegations may follow suit. . . . If Communist China is thereby voted into the United Nations over our objections we will suffer another resounding and profoundly embarrassing diplomatic setback.[62]

Not quite sure what, in this case, should be done about Nationalist China, Bowles came up with the suggestion earlier advanced by Quincy Wright, that a plebiscite be forced upon Taiwan as a result of which, it was expected, the indigenous Taiwanese would renounce their ties with China and proclaim independence. Aware, however, that such a proposal had no chance of success, Bowles said:

> It is unlikely that either Mao Tse-tung or Chiang Kai-shek would agree at this stage to abide by such plebiscite even if it were held. But American advocacy of the historic right of self-determination would place us in an unassailable position in the UN and thereby bring our own policies into closer harmony with those of our friends and our potential friends. A skilled American diplomacy and the pressure of world opinion might even make agreement on such a solution ultimately feasible.[63]

Two years later Bowles repeated his proposal in an article publish in *Foreign Affairs*. His views were considered important enough to warrant a sharp rebuttal by Chou En-lai, Prime-Minister of the Peking government, who said:

> The publication of this article not only aroused the opposition of the Chinese people on the mainland, but also arounsed the opposition of the Chinese people in Taiwan. A Hong-Kong newspaper under the influence of Taiwan said that, on the "two Chinas" question, the Republican party took a passive attitude of waiting, while the Democrats were actively taking the initiative. . . . The heart of Bowles' proposal was that the United States should work for an independent "Sino-Formosan nation." Bowles himself admitted that his scheme would probably be opposed not only by mainland China, but also by the Kuomintang in Taiwan and the Chinese in Taiwan. Therefore, such an approach would lead nowhere, but in the solution of Sino-U.S. relations, it would tie things up in knots.[64]

In a later statement, Chou En-lai reiterated the position of his government and demanded, that:

> The United Nations must expel the Chiang Kai-shek clique and restore China's legitimate rights, otherwise it will be impossible for China to have anything to do with the United Nations.[65]

Since the "two Chinas" solution has been turned down by the government of Communist China, some of the American critics have tried to invent something more acceptable. For instance, James P. Warburg on January 20, 1961, proposed the creation of an "independent Republic of Taiwan, ruled not by the refugee Chinese Nationalists but by the native Taiwanese." Warburg reasoned, that "if an independent republic were established by free plebiscite, [the refugee Chinese] would have the choice of remaining as citizens or returning to China. Those not acceptable to either country could be given asylum elsewhere."[66] Thus Warburg sought to sweeten a proposal based on that of the separation of China and Taiwan by ruling out, even before a plebiscite, a continuation of the Nationalist regime. Two months later Warburg repeated this proposal, stressing that "the two million Nationalists on Taiwan were not invited; that they seized Taiwan and are governing it as a province which they have lost." And he formulated a four point program:

1. Peking's acceptance of the Taiwanese people's right to self-determination. . . .
2. Peking's reaffirmation of its 1955 Bandung pledge to renounce force and not interfere in the internal affairs of other nations.
3. Peking's acceptance of membership in the U.N. and of a commitment to cooperate toward halting the arms race and toward the achievement of universal disarmament. . . .
4. Taiwanese agreement that, pending universal disarama-ment, an independent Republic of Taiwan would ac-cept neutralization under United Nations protection. . . .[67]

This program implies a withdrawal of the American forces from the Taiwan area and a cessation of our military aid to Taiwan (in exchange for "neutralization under United Nations protection"). Although it offers more from Peking's point of view, it still is un-likely to be accepted by Peking and is certain to be rejected by the Nationalists who, after all, exercise a very effective control over the island. William R. Frye says:

Nationalist China would acquiesce [to United Nations control] only if the alternative were imminent ejection from the United Nations and/or imminent capture by the mainland [Chinese]; and in either of those cases, Red China would scarcely wish to be deprived of the triumph she was about to win.[68]

The Nationalist position on "two Chinas" was expressed by President Chiang Kai-shek in the interview published on June 17, 1961, in *National Review*:

The so-called "two China" concept is, to put it bluntly, only wishful thinking entertained by neutralists who hope to achieve peace without paying any price for it. Our friends. . . must realize that the existence of free China is based upon the conviction that free society must in the end triumph over the Communist system of slavery. The "two China" theory totally negates this conviction and would, therefore, deprive free China of the only basis on which its sacred mission could be carried out. Here it should be very clear that the "two China'" theory, whether or not accepted by the Peiping regime, would in effect facilitate the Chinese Communists in their attempt to destroy free China.

This apparent deadlock does not discourage those who strive for accommodation with the communist bloc. One suspects that they do not truly believe that a solution satisfactory to all concerned is possible. At times, indeed, one gets an impression that all that preoccupies them is finding a kind of face-saving device which would permit them to dispose of the "Chiang Kai-shek clique" once and for all. Let us look, for example at what Professor John K. Fairbank suggested recently:

> By next September it may be impossible — or not worth the try — to prevent the United Nations Assembly voting in Red China. In any case, sooner or later, our China policy must meet two complex problems — how to bring Communist China further into an international order, and how to give Nationalist China on Taiwan a more secure international status. Both these feats must be performed soon, at the same time and in the teeth of Chinese opposition. . . . We hope to see mankind survive through arms control, for which purpose Communist China will eventually have to be included in the international order. In any case, facing the prospect that a United Nations majority may swing against our present negative stand on Red China, we need to recapture the initiative with a more flexible and creative approach. [Many considerations] have led to the so-called "two Chinas" policy, which at first step would give both Nationalist China and Communist China seats in the United Nations Assembly. Unfortunately, Chinese of both camps, all creeds, and every area denounce a "two Chinas" policy and vehemently assert they will have none of it.[69]

Fairbank, whose reputation in most quarters as a "China expert" is very high, further argues that "the phrase 'two Chinas' is in fact invidious and derogatory. It is implicitly opposed both to the modern sentiment of Chinese nationalism and to the great tradition of China's cultural-political unity." For the Chinese people, says Fairbank, "there is only one China, and considerations of the international order, arms control and human survival are quite secondary to the age-old question, who shall rule the unified

121

Chinese state." And here Fairbank comes up with a remarkable proposal:

> Instead of imposing the obnoxious term "two Chinas" from the outside, we might better describe the situation realistically in Chinese terms as one of Peking's "suzerainty" and Taipei's "autonomy". . . . Rebellious provinces of China [in the past] have also used these terms. In fact, such "autonomous" areas have behaved for long periods independently. . . yet acknowledgement of the principle of the Chinese central government's "suzerainty" has had some value for the future. . . . Taiwan today is "autonomous", in this peculiar Chinese sense of the term; that is, an independent state, as all the world can see.[70]

The practical implications of this "solution" are clear. If Taiwan is recognized as an "autonomous" province of China and nothing more the United States has no obligation to protect it and is free to abrogate the Mutual Defense treaty with that "province". Another implication is that provinces, no matter how "autonomous" (excepting the Ukraine and Bielorussia, autonomous provinces of the Soviet Union) are not entitled to representation in the United Nations. Though Fairbank avoids dotting his "i's", there is no room for misunderstanding the drift of this argument.

Such a proposal probably represents the minimum to which the Peking leaders might agree. For obvious reasons, it is unlikely to be accepted by Chiang Kai-shek or, for that matter, by the United States. As Hugh Seaton-Watson has pointed out:

> No American President could agree to what amounts to using American armed forces to destroy Chiang Kai-shek, kick him out and hand Formosa over to China. The most that any American President could do would be to recognize Communist China, have diplomatic relations with it, but leave Formosa separate.[71]

The argument of "inevitability" of Communist China's admission to the United Nations seems to have gained in popularity after the victory of the Democratic party in the 1960 elections. Adlai E. Stevenson, the new United States ambassador to the United Nations, although denying that he "had ever advocated Peiping's entrance into the international body" said that "it might be impossible to prevent" such a development.[72]

122

The talk of "inevitability" of American defeat in the United Nations on the Chinese issue immediately provoked numerous newspaper and radio-TV comments. The old cleavage in American politics, which caused so much embarrassment to the Truman administration in 1949-50 seemed to be up, once again. On January 25, 1961, it was reported that in one of his talks with the President-elect, President Eisenhower had warned Mr. Kennedy, that "if your administration tries to change the China policy that we held to, then I'm going to speak up."[73] The Committee of One Million, headed by Ambassadors Warren R. Austin and Joseph C. Grew and Senators Paul H. Douglas and Kenneth B. Keating, on February 19 announced that 54 Senators and 285 House members had joined with them in a declaration stating that "Red China had defied the U.N. Charter and [that] admitting the Peiping government to the world organization would betray the letter, violate the spirit, and subvert the purposes of that Charter."[74]

The "inevitability" approach identified with some spokesmen of the new administration was taken abroad as a hint that the United States might quit the fight. This prospect dismayed some and cheered others. On February 8, the British Foreign Office declared that the "facts of international life require Communist China's entry into the United Nations."[75] The next day the Department of State hastened to warn that the British declaration was "not a result of any consultation between our two governments."[76]

Yet, despite this denial, the State Department's statement contained an indication that the official position on the Chinese issue had undergone a major change. For the first time, the absence of Peking's representatives in the United Nations was blamed solely on the "cold, hard fact of Communist China's own attitude." Thus the United States government seemed to indicate that, if it were not for the Chinese Communists' intransigence in demanding the expulsion of the "Chiang Kai-shek clique," it would not object to the occupation by Peking of "China's rightful place" in the United Nations. This could mean only one thing — that the "two Chinas" solution of the Chinese representation issue would be attempted by the new administration. What looked like a trial balloon was launched by Eleanor Roosevelt, a member of the American United Nations delegation, when she suggested that, pending a solution of the issue, the representative of the Republic of China vacate China's permanent seat in the Security Council. This action created the impression that the United States believed that this seat had been occupied by Dr. T. F. Tsiang wrongly.

An apparent abandonment, by the United States, of firm opposition to the appearance of Communist China in the United Nations provoked a flurry of diplomatic exchanges, with a number of countries anxious to find out in what direction the United States was heading. Is a "two Chinas" policy — unrealistic as it may be — only a propaganda move, with the purpose of allowing the United States to blame the deadlock on "Communist China's own attitude?" Or is it a step towards further modification of the American stand, a modification along the lines suggested by Messrs. Warburg and Fairbank? Will the United States abandon its effort to line up enough votes in the General Assembly and exercise its right of veto in the Security Council in order to block the seating of the Chinese Communists? A somewhat vague answer to these questions was supplied by Secretary of State Rusk, at his news-conference of March 9, 1961:

> If this matter is treated as purely a credentials question, as a question as to which delegation sits in a particular seat. . . then we should have a very serious problem indeed. On the other hand, the authorities in Peiping have made it clear over and over again that if any recognition. . . is given to the Government of the Republic of China on Formosa that they would not accept any solution that involved that result. So, this is a complex question. It has far-reaching ramifications, which go far beyond the technical question of credentials.[77]

In other words, Rusk reserves for the United States the right to veto the entry of Communist China in the Security Council and to demand a ⅔ majority in the General Assembly vote on the issue. Commenting the same day in *The New York Times*, William J. Jorden wrote:

> Peiping's apparently inflexible stand precludes any quick or easy answers to the problem of China's future role in the United Nations. [It is believed in Washington] that a majority of member nations are not prepared to see the liquidation of Nationalist China and that Peiping will

accept nothing less. . . . The question of Peiping's entry to the United Nations may prove to be academic.[78]

Although the open concession of the "inevitability" of Peking's entry into the United Nations has since ceased in official circles, speculations at home and abroad have continued. Great Britain has apparently committed itself to press for the seating of Communist China in the 16th session of the General Assembly, even at the risk of a collision with the United States. President Quadros of Brazil announced that his government will favor a full debate of the issue.

Although most of the new administration's diplomatic activities in "sensitive" areas have been carried on in secret, enough has appeared on the surface to indicate that a major reappraisal of United States policy in Asia is in the making. Following a "deal" with the Soviet chief representative, Adlai E. Stevenson, the head of the American delegation, refrained from traditional accusations of the Chinese Communists during the discussion of the Tibet issue. He also sought to prevent the appearance of the Laotian crisis on the agenda of the General Assembly and the Security Council, and avoided putting even a part of the blame for the aggression in Laos on the Peking regime. A "package deal" was worked out with the Soviets whereby Outer Mongolia could be admitted to membership simultaneously with Mauritania, whose admission had been blocked by a Soviet veto. At the same time, in secret negotiations in Moscow, the United States offered diplomatic recognition to Outer Mongolia, the least independent of all communist satellites, recognized by a mere twenty other countries. These moves were approved by the Soviet Union which would not miss a chance to add an extra vote to its bloc of votes in the General Assembly.

The "fresh look" further manifested itself by the administration's initiative in proposing an exchange of newsmen with Peking. Here, however, the American overtures were rebuked by the Peking leadership which, promptly turning down the proposal, and reiterated its demand that the Taiwan issue be settled to its satisfaction prior to the discussion of any other question.

Alarmed by all these steps, a group of congressmen introduced, on May 3, 1961, in both houses of Congress, a resolution expressing continuing American opposition to recognition of Communist China and to its seating in the United Nations. Under the pressure of Democratic leadership this resolution was pigeonholed in the respective foreign relations committees, despite known majorities favoring its approval in both the Senate and the House of Representatives Foreign Relations Committee. It was later brought to the Senate floor and approved unanimously.

On June 24, *The New York Times* reported that the United States government was studying the possibility of offering Communist China representation in the General Assembly, and that Harlan Cleveland, Assistant Secretary of State for International Organizations, was making a tour in Europe, discussing with American allies the ways of effecting the "two Chinas" solution in the United Nations. Adlai E. Stevenson was reported to have discussed the same subject during his trip in Latin America. The reported presumption behind the move was that Peking would reject the proposal, thereby freeing the United States from any responsibility for its absence from the United Nations.

The Republicans in the Senate immediately accused the State Department of "playing Russian roulette" with China policy and demanded a vote on the May 3, 1961, resolution. J. W. Fulbright, chairman of the Senate Foreign Relations Committee, replied that he saw no reason for hasty action on the resolution.

On July 2, *The New York Times* published a report that preliminary polls in United Nations circles indicated the inevitability of a full debate of the Chinese representation issue at the General Assembly session next September, but that American officials do not concede yet that they have lost the votes necessary to postpone the discussion.

An Associated Press dispatch from Taiwan carried in the *New York Herald-Tribune* on July 6 reported Premier Chen Cheng's declaration that "if the situation is not favorable to us, we will withdraw from the United Nations." Whether he meant the General Assembly only or also a withdrawal from the Security Council, remained unclear. The same report revealed that the "fresh look" at the China policy has already brought about a major crisis in Washington's relations with the Republic of China and that the American ambassador in Taiwan was coming to Washington for "urgent consultations."

On the same day, Lincoln White, the State Department's press-officer, described as "inaccurate" reports that the United States was considering a "two Chinas" proposal on the assumption that the Peking regime would reject it. He did not elaborate whether the government hoped for Peking's acceptance of the offer.

On July 21, the *Associated Press* reported that Everett F. Drumright, United States Ambassador to Nationalist China, said after a talk with President Kennedy that "the United States would seek a United Nations agreement keeping Nationalist China in and Communist China out of the world organization," and that he personally "did not agree with the opinion that Communist China's admission to the United Nation's General Assembly was a certainty." The report continued, that Drumright "left the impression that there had been no final decision by Mr. Kennedy on the procedure for handling the China question."

Because of the known views of some of the key officials in the government, these and other vague and contradictory statements, and press and radio reports have led to growing fear that the United States is secretly preparing its own defeat in the United Nations. The widely circulated study by the American Security Council, published in June, 1961, said:

> It is difficult to predict the outcome of a general debate on Communist China admission. However, it seems reasonable to conclude that the net result will be harmful to our loyal ally, the Nationalist Chinese; that it will add to the already confused and muddled thinking within this country which supports recognition of Red China; that it will further undermine the structure of the United Nations itself; and that it will in various ways adversely affect our strategic posture in the Far East.

The report charged that:

> Many experts in the Department of State are considering this problem not from the point of view of how to keep Communist China out of the U.N., but rather how to let them in without openly abrogating our treaty commitments to our ally. . . and without clearly ignoring the views of the American people.

In conclusion, the report urged a prompt passing of a concurrent resolution in Congress, which will (a) express our continuing opposition to Red China's membership, and (b) state clearly that if Communist China is admitted, we will have to reconsider whether it is still in our national interest to associate ourselves with the United Nations organization.

* * *

On the eve of the 16th Session of the General Assembly, the outcome of the Chinese representation issue is, indeed, difficult to predict. One thing is clear, however: if the General Assembly recommends by a two-thirds majority the seating of Communist China, it would mean the beginning of an era when the United States would find itself in a permanent minority in that organization. The failure to line up the votes necessary to prevent the passage of the resolution would be ascribed not only to the inefficiency and the half-heartedness of the administration in its handling of this affair, but also to its tacit — and not so tacit — encouragement of American allies to vote against the "official" United States stand.

The adoption of this resolution may have no direct effect, for the Peking regime would be likely to ignore it. But if Taiwan representatives carry out their "threat" and walk out, vacating China's seats in all United Nations organs, the situation would be different.

The appearance of the Peking delegation in New York could hardly be expected to pass unnoticed by the American public. The sensation it would cause might easily produce a storm which might spell a defeat of the Democratic Party in forthcoming elections. It can also be foreseen that reverberations of the affair would seriously injure the United Nations, regardless of whether the United States — and some other countries — withdraw from the world organization. With the communist bloc exerting increased influence in the United Nations, the support it receives from the West would diminish sharply and the organization would have to undergo a transformation which none of the exponents of the "United Nations point of view" would want to see.

CONCLUSIONS

As of this writing, nobody knows exactly what the United States policy toward China is. Official statements have been numerous and contradictory, and they prove — or disprove — little. We may be fairly sure that recognition of Communist China is not yet "under active consideration" in the State Department but the situation with the problem of Chinese representation in the United Nations may be different. There have been many reports from well informed sources to indicate a sharp division of opinion in the government on how the China policy is to be directed. It appears, that the career foreign service officers and the military are almost unanimously opposed to any modification of the traditional American policy in the Far East, while some of the political appointees of the new administration and the *entourage* they brought with them to the State Department and to the American delegation to the United Nations, are pushing for it. On the whole, it would be safe to say that the demands for "flexibility" in dealing with the China problem come from what is known as "liberal" circles, this small but very vocal and well organized sector of the American opinion, which got a strong foothold in the government under President Kennedy.

The President, who under the Constitution is solely responsible for the conduct of foreign affairs, is, for the time being, doubtless listening to both sides, following the arguments *for* and *against*. In his decisions he is likely to take into consideration the sentiment in the country and, particularly, in the Congress. His decisions would also probably be affected by developments in such widely separated areas as Japan, Southeast Asia, Latin America and Berlin, for he has to uphold global commitments of the United States and to develop a consistent and wholesome approach to major problems this country faces in our complex and troubled world. On the other hand, he will be influenced by the views of American allies, who are divided on the subject as sharply as are the Americans. In the end, he would act according to his own judgment.

Essentially, as we have seen, there are two ways of dealing with the China problem. One is to continue to oppose the Peking regime by all available means and on all existing fronts, including that of the United Nations. Contrary to what the critics of the American China policy have been saying, there is nothing "negativistic" in this opposition. To deny the sworn enemy the fruits of victory — and there is no question that the seating of Communist China in the United Nations would represent such — is to pursue an active and constructive policy. True, some American allies and a good many "neutrals" might be unhappy over this policy, but who would suggest that the United States should give up the fight and concede its own defeat in order to please governments whose attitude to China has been formed by their own interests, different from and sometimes opposing those of this country?

Another way is offered by advocates of the "flexible" approach who attempt to prove that accommodation with the communists is in our national interest and that such an accommodation is feasible. Their arguments remain manifestly unconvincing, for they are based on risky speculations and, most of all, on lack of knowledge of the communist *modus operandi*. Being basically pacifists — Chester Bowles' record of pacifism goes back to 1941 when he was arguing against American intervention in the war against the Nazis — they are guided more by wishful thinking than by a sober appreciation of realities. Scared by the prospect of a nuclear holocaust, they tend to adopt what amounts to a defeatist attitude in confrontation with the communists. They want accommodation because they have no will to fight. So, they delude themselves — and others — that the communist governments are not as bad as they are presumed to be and that if approached with friendliness and understanding they would be amenable. They discard entirely the endless record of unsuccessful efforts to negotiate with the communist powers, or they attribute the failure of these negotiations to a lack of appreciation on the part of the United States of communist needs. To correct the situation they propose to increase intercourse with the enemy from the summit down to the tourist level, to offer him the inducements of trade and even aid; and they propose to bring the Chinese Communists into the "community of nations" in a hope that this would make them more civil and

130

easier to deal with. One can only ask: how much has the presence of the Soviet Union and its satellites in the United Nations contributed to *their* mellowing?

The danger of the "flexible" approach is twofold. In the first place, its chances to succeed in making the communists friendlier and more relaxed are nil. In the second place, it accelerates the process of eroding the belief in values of democracy among the American people. Although some "liberals" would challenge that, from the moral point of view the communists are no better than the Nazis were. Why, then, didn't the "liberals" try to develop closer ties with the Third Reich in prewar years? Why didn't they work for greater "cultural exchanges" and "intellectual acceptability" of the Nazis? And Hitler — as Japanese militarists — was much more predisposed to stay on speaking terms with the United States than the communists are!

"Flexibility", quite obviously, is no end in itself. Few of its advocates admit it in public, but their real goal is finding an understanding with the communist powers by satisfying their "legitimate interests" — preferably at the expense of third powers — and achieving a true peaceful coexistence, perhaps through division of the world between the two camps. In that they go considerably farther than FDR did, and we know that it is largely because of the Teheran and Yalta concessions to Stalin that the communists came to represent a clear and immediate threat to the Western way of life.

In postwar years, the United States and its allies tried, for the time being, a policy of "containment" of communism. It did not solve all Western problems, for it was mainly a delaying action which in the end failed to prevent the communist political penetration of the underdeveloped world. Nonetheless, it was the best that modern democracies, inherently incapable of aggressiveness and dedicated to the preservation of the *status quo*, could offer. The "containment" policy at least made the communist gains costly and their advances limited. The weakening of the containment policy soon brought bad results. Starting with the 1955 summit meeting in Geneva, communist incursions into the Middle East, Africa, Asia and Latin America greatly increased in scope and boldness, until now, in the summer of 1961, the West finds itself pretty much cornered.

131

If the apostles of "flexibility" would have it their own way, the showdown will come sooner than all of us expect, for the communists will take full advantage of every Western concession and will press for complete victory. The seating of Communist China in the United Nations and its recognition by the United States would bring such victory that much closer.

NOTES

PART ONE

1. A. Doak Barnett, *Communist China and Asia* (N.Y., 1960), p. 430. Hereinafter to be noted as Barnett, *CC&A*.

2. Dean Acheson, "Crisis in Asia — An Examination of United States Policy," *Department of State Publication 3747*, February 1950.

3. Quincy Wright, "The Chinese Recognition Problem," *The American Journal of International Law*, Vol. 49, 1955, pp. 320-338. Hereinafter to be noted as Wright, *AJIL*.

4. Hans J. Morgenthau, *Politics Among Nations*, 3d edition, (N.Y., 1960), p. 145.

5. Even with the benefit of hindsight, Mr. Truman feels that there was no miscalculation on his part and that his line on China — whatever it was — was correct and supported by the public at large: "It is characteristic of any system where free expression of opinion prevails that the critics and the malcontents will be heard more often than those who support the established policy. . . . A President must not be influenced by this distortion of opinion. He must be able to distinguish between propaganda and the true opinion of the people." *The Memoirs of Harry S. Truman* (N.Y., 1956), p. 414.

6. Quincy Wright, *op. cit.*

7. Trygve Lie, *In the Cause of Peace* (N.Y., 1954), pp. 264-265.

8. Joseph A. Whelan, "The U.S. and Diplomatic Recognition: The Contrasting Cases of Russia and Communist China," *The China Quarterly*, No. 5, Jan.-March 1961, p. 70.

9. By January 2, 1950, all communist countries declared their recognition of the new government of China. Between December 1959 and April 1950 it was recognized by India, Burma, Indonesia, Pakistan, Ceylon, Afganistan, Sweden, Denmark, Norway, Ireland, Israel, The Netherlands and Great Britain. No further recognitions followed until 1956 when Egypt, Syria and Yemen were added to the list. Since 1959 some of the new nations extended their recognition to Peking: Guinea, Ghana, Cambodia, Mali, Sudan, Somalia and Upper Volta. This adds up to 34 nations (counting the Ukraine and Byelorussia) which are members of the United Nations. In addition, the Peking regime is recognized by Switzerland, East Germany, North Vietnam, North Korea and Outer Mongolia. This data is as of June 1961.

10. For reasons of the Communist China actions in connection with the Korean War, see Allen S. Whiting, "The Logic of Communist China Policy," *The Yale Review*, Autumn 1960.

11. Actually, too little is known about what went on in the government's policy-making circles during that period to draw any definite conclusions. What has been published so far has had unreasonably strong partisan overtones. Allen S. Whiting's recent book on the Korean War provides some plausible — though speculative — answers.

12. Quincy Wright, "The Status of Communist China," *Journal of International Affairs*, Vol. XI, No. 2, 1957. Hereinafter noted as Wright, *JIA*.

13. Lauterpacht, *Recognition*, p. 24. Quoted by Wright, *op. cit.*

14. Lauterpacht, *op. cit.*, p. 94. Quoted by Stanley K. Hornbeck, "Recogni-

tion of Governments," *The American Society of International Law Proceedings*, April 1950.

15. L. Oppenheim, *International Law*, Vol. 1, p. 136. Quoted, among others, by Walton Moore, in memorandum of October 4, 1933, Foreign Relations Series, "The Soviet Union 1933-1939" (Washington, 1952), *Department of State Publication 4539*, p. 136.

16. Ti-Chiang Chen, *The International Law of Recognition*, (London, 1951), p. 99.

17. *Ibid.*, p. 118.

18. Stanley K. Hornbeck, "Which Chinese?," *Foreign Affairs*, Vol. 34, No. 1, October 1955. Hereinafter noted as Hornbeck, "Which Chinese?"

19. John Foster Dulles, "Our Policies Toward Communism in China," Address, June 28, 1957, *The Department of State Bulletin*, Vol. XXXVII, No. 942, July 15, 1957. Hereinafter noted as Dulles, "Our Policies".

20. Pitman B. Potter, "Editorial Comment," *The American Journal of International Law*, Vol. 50, 1956, p. 417.

21. See Jefferson's note to Gouvernor Morris, March 12, 1793 (Moore, *Digest*, Vol, I, p. 120). An interpretation, according to which Jefferson meant here a test of democratic popularity of a government is questioned by T. C. Chen: "To the present writer, it seems that Jefferson had merely laid down a principle, and not prescribed a test. A democratic test would ill accord with his subsequent opinion that kings and conventions are equally entitled to recognition." *Op. cit.*, p. 122.

22. "When during the spring of 1957, mainland middle-school and college students staged demonstrations *in every province*, many of them voiced support for the Nationalists." Richard L. Walker, "The U.S. Should Not Change its China Policy," *Headline Series*, No. 129, May-June 1958, p. 56. In support of his view, Walker further points out that over 5,000 Chinese, mostly peasants, escape monthly to Hong Kong.

23. Wright, *JIA*.

24. John King Fairbank, *The United States and China*, (Harvard University Press, 1959), p. 319.

25. David Nelson Rowe, *Modern China*, (D. Van Nostrand Co., Princeton, N.J., 1959), p. 97.

26. K. C. Wheare, *Federal Government*, (Oxford University Press, 1953), p. 192. Wheare quotes Corwin's *The President: Office and Powers*, p. 322.

27. "United States Policy on Nonrecognition of Communist China," Press Release, August 11, 1958, *The Department of State Bulletin*, Vol. XXXIX, No. 1002, September 8, 1958. Hereinafter to be noted as *State, Major*.

28. Dean Rusk, Speech before the China Institute in America, May 18, 1951. It has to be noted, however, that Rusk's speech caused some embarrassment to Acheson who, while endorsing the "substance" of it, expressed his disagreement with its "wording". See *The New York Times*, June 6, 1951.

29. Walter S. Robertson, "Meeting the Threat of Communism in the Far East," *The Department of State Bulletin*, Vol. XXXVI, No. 922, February 25, 1957. Other sources give higher estimates. Paul K. T. Sih gives figures of 30 million executed and 90 million sent to concentration camps in 1949-1959. The Nationalist sources on Taiwan are apt to give even higher estimates. A figure of 9 million executed was once reported in official Chinese Communist publications.

30. Memorandum of July 19, 1923, by Secretary of State Hughes, quoted in Hackworth, *Digest of International Law*, Vol. I, p. 198.

31. Arthur H. Dean, Note on Diplomatic Recognition of Governments in "The United States and the Far East," *The American Assembly, School of Business*, Columbia University, 1956.

32. Arthur H. Dean, "United States Policy and Formosa," *Foreign Affairs*, Vol. 33, No. 3, April 1955.

134

33. Wright, *JIA*.
34. T. C. Chen, *op. cit.*, p. 78.
35. Arthur H. Dean, "Note on Diplomatic Recognition," etc., *op. cit.*
36. Barnett, *CC&A*, p. 435.
37. Wright, *JIA*.
38. T. C. Chen, *op. cit.*, p. 126.
39. Barnett, *CC&A*, p. 434.
40. Dulles, "Our Policies."
41. *State, Major*.
42. Dulles, "Our Policies."
43. *Ibid*.
44. See Note 14.
45. Percy E. Corbett, "National Interest, International Organization and American Foreign Policy," *World Politics*, Vol. V, No. 1, October 1952.
46. Hornbeck, "Which Chinese?"
47. John Foster Dulles, "Press Conference," *The Department of State Bulletin*, Vol. XXXVIII, No. 971, February 3, 1958, p. 165.
48. John Foster Dulles, "Statement on United States China Policy," March 12, 1957, *The Department of State Bulletin*, Vol. XXVI, No. 927, April 1957.
49. *State, Major*.
50. Hornbeck, "Which Chinese?"
51. See Note 20.
52. Myres S. McDougal, "Some Basic Theoretical Concepts about International Law," *Conflict Resolution*, Vol. IV, No. 3, September 1960.
53. William K. Knowland, "The United States Should Not Recognize Communist China," *Journal of International Affairs*, Vol. XI, No. 2, 1957.
54. Paul H. Douglas, "What Are America's Interests in the Issue of Recognizing Red China?" *Free China & Asia*, Vol. VI, No. 9, September 1959.
55. Pitman B. Potter, *op. cit.*, p. 418.
56. Barnett, *CC&A*, p. 442.
57. Committee on Foreign Relations, U.S. Senate, 86th Congress, 1st Session. Asia: Studies Prepared by Conlon Associates, Ltd., Washington, GPO, 1959, p. 147. Hereinafter noted as *Conlon Report*.
58. *Ibid.*, p. 154.
59. Walter S. Robertson, *op. cit.*
60. *State, Major*.
61. Dulles, "Our Policies".
62. Barnett, *CC&A*, p. 441.
63. Rowe, *op. cit.*, p. 98.
64. Paul K. T. Sih, "Should We Recognize Red China?" *The New World*, Chicago, April 8, 1960.
65. *Ibid*.
66. Edgar Snow, quoting Chou En-lai, in "A Report from Red China," *Look*, January 31, 1961, Vol. 25, No. 3.
67. J. Graham Parsons, *The American Role in Pacific-Asian Affairs*, Address, February 19, 1960, published by the Committee of One Million, New York, 1960.
68. *The New York Times*, March 4, 1961.
69. As of the spring of 1961, of the 13 countries of the Far East and Southeast Asia, only four had recognized Communist China.
70. *The New York Times*, March 9, 1961.
71. Barnett, *CC&A*, p. 443.
72. Richard L. Walker, *op. cit.*, p. 66.
73. *Ibid.*, p. 67.
74. *Conlon Report*, p. 149.
75. *Ibid.*, p. 137.

76. Barnett, *CC&A*, p. 445.

77. Philip E. Mosely, *Moscow-Peking Axis: Strengths and Strains*, (N.Y., 1957). Quoted by Eustace Seligman, "The U.S. Should Change Its China Policy," *Headline Series*, No. 129, May- June 1958.

78. Robertson, *op. cit.*

79. Thomas K. Finletter, *Foreign Policy: The Next Phase*, (N.Y., 1958).

80. Barnett, *CC&A*, p. 456.

81. *State, Major.*

82. Dulles, "Our Policies".

83. Barnett, *CC&A*, p. 435.

84. *Ibid.*, p. 436.

85. *Ibid.*, p. 442.

86. The evidence demonstrating this attitude is overwhelming. For our purposes, the Snow report in *Look* is sufficient, for its accuracy cannot be questioned.

87. Rowe, *op. cit.*, p. 97.

88. Snow, *op. cit.*

89. Thomas E. Murray, "Nuclear Testing and American Security," *ORBIS*, Vol. IV, No. 4, Winter 1961.

90. Chester Bowles, *The Coming Political Breakthrough*, (N.Y., 1959), p. 155.

91. A. Doak Barnett, "The Inclusion of Communist China in Arms Control Program," DAEDALUS, Fall 1960, pp. 831-845.

92. *Ibid.*

93. Henry A. Kissinger, *The Necessity for Choice* (N.Y., 1961), p. 272.

94. James E. Dougherty, "Key to Security: Disarmament or Arms Stability?" *ORBIS*, Vol. IV, Fall 1960, pp. 261-283.

95. Morgenthau, *op. cit.*, p. 411.

96. See Kennan's testimony before the Jackson Committee, United States Senate, May 7, 1960. Quoted by Seligman, *op. cit.*

97. Emery Reves, "Why Waste Time Discussing Disarmament?" *Look*, March 28, 1961, Vol. 25, No. 7.

98. Chester Bowles, "The 'China Problem' Reconsidered," *Foreign Affairs*, Vol. 38, No. 3, April 1960.

99. See Note 90.

100. Christian Herter, "Remarks", *Department of State Press Release* No. 667, September 23, 1959, p. 7.

101. Oskar Morgenstern, "The N Country Problem", *Fortune*, March 1961.

102. *Ibid.*

103. Utilization of the disarmament issue for the purposes of getting Communist China into the United Nations is discussed by Lincoln P. Bloomfield, *The United Nations and U.S. Foreign Policy*, (Boston, 1960), pp. 251-252. Such utilization is strongly objected to by the opposition. For instance, American Security Council, a private organization which includes a number of prominent military leaders now in retirement, in its special Washington Report of June 1961, declares: "the pious hope that by making Communist China a member of the U.N. would force her to bow to the pressures of world opinion and abide by both the spirit and the letter of international agreements, is hardly a sound basis for the reduction of armaments. In fact, if anything, the admission of another Communist state would make it possible for the bloc to take an even more rigid and belligerent position on all disarmament matters."

104. Marvin L. Kalb, *Dragon in The Kremlin*, (N.Y. 1961), p. 249.

105. *State, Major.*

106. Hans Kelsen, *Recent Trends in the Law of the United Nations* (London, 1951), p. 947.

107. Whelan, *op. cit.*, p. 77.

108. Snow, *op. cit.*
109. Barnett, *CC&A*, p. 451.
110. Snow, *op. cit.*
111. *Ibid.*
112. *Ibid.*
113. *Ibid.*
114. Rowe, in *American Political Science Review,* Vol. LIV, No. 4, December 1960.
115. Dean,, in *Foreign Affairs, op. cit.*
116. *Conlon Report,* p. 136.
117. Finletter, *op. cit.,* p. 163.
118. *Ibid.,* p. 164.
119. Wright, *AJIL.*
120. Finletter, *op. cit.,* p. 122.
121. Fairbank, *op. cit.,* p. 277.
122. Snow, *op. cit.*
123. Whiting in *The Yale Review, op. cit.*
124. Paul M. A. Linebarger, *Journal of International Affairs,* Vol. XI, No. 2, 1957.
125. *Conlon Report,* p. 145.
126. Hugh Seaton-Watson, Interview in the *U.S. News & World Report,* October 24, 1960.
127. Linebarger, *op. cit.*
128. Rowe, in *American Political Science Review, op. cit.*
129. *State, Major.*
130. Morgenthau, "The Yardstick of National Interest", *The Annals of The American Society of Political and Social Science,* November 1954.
131. Snow, *op. cit.*
132. *Conlon Report,* p. 138.
133. Barnett, *CC&A*, p. 437.
134. *Ibid.*
135. Dean, in *Foreign Affairs, op. cit.*
136. *Conlon Report,* p. 137.
137. Barnett, *CC&A*, p. 460.
138. *Ibid.,* p. 461.
139. *Conlon Report,* p. 148.
140. See, for instance, H. Arthur Steiner's essay, "Communist China in The World Community", *International Conciliation,* No. 533, May, 1961.
141. Fairbank, *op. cit.,* p. 3.
142. *Ibid.,* p. 317.
143. *Conlon Report,* pp. 134-135.
144. *Journal of International Affairs,* Vol. XI, No. 2, 1957.
145. Bloomfield, *op. cit.,* p. 129.
146. Finletter, *op. cit.,* p. 160.
147. Bowles, *Ideas, People and Peace* (N.Y., 1958), p. 84.
148. Kalb, *op. cit.,* pp. 248-249.
149. *Ibid.,* p. 250.
150. *Ibid.,* p. 251.
151. Mosely, *op. cit.*
152. William J. Jorden, "Soviet-Chinese Split?" *The New York Times,* November 13, 1960.
153. *State, Major.*
154. Kissinger, *op. cit.,* p. 202.
155. Snow, *op. cit.*
156. See "China's Threat to Russia", the *New Leader,* April 24, 1961.
157. Suzanne Labin and Christopher Emmet, "Is There a Sino-Soviet Split?" *ORBIS,* Vol. IV, No. 1, Spring 1960.

137

158. Paul Wohl, "Red Bloc Split or Fraud?" *The Christian Science Monitor*, February 14, 1961.

159. *Ibid.*

160. W. W. Rostow, *The Prospects for Communist China*, (N.Y., 1954), p. 219.

161. Dulles, "Our Policies".

162. Kalb, *op. cit.*, p. 251.

163. Such an assumption invariably leads the critics to place the blame with the West. For instance, Professor H. Arthur Steiner states: "No one can say whether the CPR (the Chinese People's Republic) would have followed a more moderate course in international affairs after 1950 had it been saved the aggravation of Taiwan. Is it not quite possible that with an integrated territory and an assured security the Chinese Communist leaders would have concentrated more of their energies on the gigantic tasks of internal revolutionary transformation, and have been less disposed to adventuristic policies in foreign affairs? As it happened, however, they exploited the menace of external attack, . . . and judged that there could be no complete victory on the domestic front without complete victory on the foreign front." "Communist China in the World Community", *International Conciliation* no. 533, p. 391, May 1961. Professor Steiner misses entirely the point that the main "aggravation" of the communist powers is the very existence of the Western world. The fact that the Soviet Union possesses both an "integrated territory" and all the "assured security" it can ask for, does not make it less disposed to "adventuristic policies in foreign affairs" although there is plenty that has to be done in solving its "gigantic tasks of internal revolutionary transformation". Steiner's suggestion that denial of Taiwan to Communist China represents a "menace of external attack" is too farfetched to be taken seriously.

164. On July 8, 1961, *The New York Times* published a letter by a Henry S. Huntington from Philadelphia, saying: "How very nice it would be if the United States would grow up! Specifically grow up to the point of maturity where we should recognize that China — 'Mainland China' as both naive and artful-minded people like to call it — is really China and one of the great powers in this world — indeed one of the very greatest. Why don't we get over the farce of insisting on the little island of Formosa being a member of the Security Council of the United Nations, endowed, moreover with the tremendous power of the veto!"

165. W. W. Rostow, *op. cit.*, p. 52.

166. *Ibid.*, p. 53.

167. Snow, *op. cit.*

168. Whelan, *op. cit.*, p. 67.

169. Parsons, *op. cit.*

170. Whelan, *op. cit.*, p. 69.

171. Steiner, *op. cit.*

172. Barnett, *CC&A*, p. 469.

173. Whelan, *op. cit.*, p. 67.

174. Chester Bowles, *Ideas, People and Peace*, p. 140.

175. Washington Report, American Security Council, Special Issue, June 1961.

176. For a full story of recognition of Soviet Russia, see Robert Paul Browder's *The Origins of Soviet-American Diplomacy*, Princeton University Press, 1953.

177. Whelan, *op. cit.*, p. 64.

178. *Ibid.*

179. *Ibid.*, p. 65.

180. *Ibid.*

181. *Ibid.*

182. *Ibid.*, p. 85.
183. Rowe, in the *American Political Science Review, op. cit.*
184. Bowles, *Ideas,* etc., *op. cit.*, p. 142.
185. Whelan, *op. cit.*, p. 86.
186. Dulles, "Our Policies".

PART TWO

1. Gross said: "I wish to make it clear that my government will accept the decision of the Security Council on this matter when made by an affirmative vote of seven members." S/PV.460, p. 6.
2. S/PV. 459, 460, 461, January 10-13, 1950. *Also:* Annual Report of the Secretary-General (A/1287) for 1949-1950, pp. 31-33; *also:* Report of the Security Council (A/1361) pp. 51-57.
3. Security Council document S/1466, March 9, 1950.
4. Security Council document S/1470, March 15, 1950.
5. Trygve Lie, *In the Cause of Peace,* (N.Y., 1954), pp. 265-266.
6. Security Council document S/PV.480/ Rev.1, August 1, 1950, p. 1.
7. General Assembly document A/1308, August 4, 1950.
8. General Assembly resolution 396(V) A/PV.325, December 14, 1950, p. 675.
9. Herbert W. Briggs, "Chinese Representation in the United Nations," *International Organization,* May 1952, p. 206.
10. By a vote of 44:7 (Soviet bloc countries, India, Burma), with 9 abstentions. General Assembly document A/PV.327, February 1, 1951.
11. By a vote of 44:0, with 8 abstentions. The Soviet bloc countries did not participate in voting.
12. Dean Rusk, Speech Before the China Institute in America, May 18, 1951. Published by the Committee of One Million.
13. The statement was made by Acheson during the Gen. MacArthur hearings in the Senate on June 6, 1951. Acheson also expressed a belief that the World Court ruling would be desirable on applicability of veto in this case. It should be noted that the Rusk statement (see note 12 above) created great furor and that on June 5, 1951 Acheson announced that in the future all statements dealing with foreign policy would have to be cleared with him. Nonetheless, he expressed his agreement with the "substance" of the Rusk speech.
14. General Assembly document A/PV.342, November 13, 1951, pp. 99-104, and Report of the General Committee, document A/1950, November 10, 1951. Fred Greene says: "Only since 1953 has Russian pressure been relaxed to the point where the matter, though still brought up, could quickly be disposed of in routine fashion. . . . Earlier. . . the United States was confronted with the wearisome chore of clearing a statement with both Britain and Nationalist China, and then carrying this through a UN committee session with carefully arranged, technically correct parliamentary procedures. . . . The American Mission was under constant instruction to marshal a majority vote at various sessions. Concentration on success required a meticulous preparation on all aspects of this question by the Delegation. More commonly, it required careful tabulation of the likely outcome of the vote and, when necessary, lobbying to get friendly delegations to be on hand." Fred Greene, *Chinese Representation: a Case Study in United Nations Political Affairs,* Part II, Woodrow Wilson Foundation, (N.Y., 1955).
15. Egon F. Ranshofen-Wertheimer, *The International Secretariat,* (Carnegie Foundation for International Peace, 1945), p. 249.
16. Briggs, *op. cit.*, p. 193.

17. Hans Kelsen, *Recent Trends in the Law of the United Nations*, London, 1951, p. 943.

18. Briggs, *op. cit.*, p. 209.

19. Greene, *op. cit.*, p. 38.

20. Briggs, *op. cit.*, p. 206.

21. Walter S. Robertson, "Meeting the Threat of Communism in the Far East," *The Department of State Bulletin*, XXXVI, No. 922, February 25, 1957.

22. General Assembly document A/1844/Add.1

23. A. Doak Barnett, *Communist China and Asia*, (N.Y., 1960), p. 449.

24. In the United Nations the British took a legalistic view of the situation. Trying to bypass both formal and political tests which the Chinese representation issue had to meet, Sir Frank Soskice led a fight in the First Committee. He said that moral or political judgments on such matters as willingness to fulfil international obligations might be appropriate only to questions of *admission* or *expulsion* of members. The position of the British government was that no moral tests are applicable when the issue is that of *representation*, that China *already* was a member of the United Nations and that the only practicable test was the factual and objective test of the effectiveness of the government. See General Assembly document A/AC38/SR 18, October 20, 1950, pp. 116-117.

25. John Foster Dulles, Statement on US China Policy, March 12, 1957, *The Department of State Bulletin*, XXVI, No. 927, April 1, 1957.

26. U.S. Policy on Nonrecognition of Communist China, August 11, 1958, *The Department of State Bulletin*, XXXIX, No. 1002, September 8, 1958.

27. John Foster Dulles, Our Policies Toward Communism in China, Address, June 28, 1957, *The Department of State Bulletin*, XXXVII, No. 942, July 15, 1957.

28. Briggs, *op. cit.*, p. 195.

29. Lincoln P. Bloomfield, *The United Nations and U.S. Foreign Policy*, (Boston, 1960), p. 122.

30. Kelsen, *op. cit.*, p. 947.

31. *Ibid.*

32. For instance, take the State Department's statement saying that "recognition of Peiping by the United States would inevitably lead to the seating of Peiping in the United Nations". See note 26.

33. Pitman B. Potter, Editorial Comment, *American Journal of International Law*, v. 50, 1956, p. 418.

34. Inis Claude, *Swords into Plowshares*, (N.Y., 1956), p. 104.

35. Kelsen, *op. cit.*, p. 945.

36. *Ibid.*, p. 946. The Heads or Foreign Ministers of Member States are not required to have *any* credentials.

37. *Ibid.*, p. 947.

38. Greene, *op. cit.*, p. 35.

39. Briggs, *op. cit.*, p. 195.

40. *Ibid.*

41. "It must be admitted. . . that another interpretation according to which such approval has no legal effect on the Members, is not excluded." Kelsen, *op. cit.*, p. 948.

42. *Ibid.*, p. 944.

43. *Ibid.*, pp. 946-947.

44. Greene, *op. cit.*, p. 50.

45. Claude, *op. cit.*, p. 102.

46. Hans J. Morgenthau, "The Yardstick of National Interest", *The Annals of the American Society of Political and Social Science*, November, 1954.

47. Greene, *op. cit.*, p. 34.

48. Barnett, *op. cit.*, p. 488.